THE AUDUBON SOCIETY

by Les Line, *Editor of Audubon magazine, and Edward R. Ricciuti*

A Chanticleer Press Edition

BOOK OF WILD CATS

HARRY N. ABRAMS, INC., PUBLISHERS, NEW YORK

Library of Congress Cataloging in Publication Data
Line, Les.
The Audubon Society book of wild cats.
"A Chanticleer Press edition."
Includes index.
1. Felidae.   I. Ricciuti, Edward R.   II. National
Audubon Society.   III. Title.
QL737.C23L552   1985   599.74'428   84-18475
ISBN 0-8109-1828-5
Published in 1985 by Harry N. Abrams, Incorporated, New York.

Trademark "Audubon Society" used by publisher under license by the
National Audubon Society, Inc.

Prepared and produced by Chanticleer Press, Inc.
Manufactured in Japan

Chanticleer Staff
Publisher: Paul Steiner
Editor-in-Chief: Gudrun Buettner
Managing Editor: Susan Costello
Senior Editor: Mary Beth Brewer
Assistant Editor: David Allen
Production: Helga Lose, Amy Roche
Art Director: Carol Nehring
Art Associate: Ayn Svoboda
Picture Library: Edward Douglas, Dana Pomfret
Natural Science Consultant: John Farrand, Jr.
Design: Massimo Vignelli

First frontispiece: *A tiger* (Panthera tigris) *in full stride.*
(Guenter Ziesler)
Second frontispiece: *A caracal* (Felis caracal) *retreats from
an encounter with a cheetah* (Acinonyx jubatus). (Mitch
Reardon/Photo Researchers, Inc.)
Third frontispiece: *A lion* (Panthera leo) *in hot pursuit of
a zebra on the Masai Mara of Kenya.* (Guenter Ziesler)
Fourth frontispiece: *A tiger drags a freshly killed sambar
deer from a marsh in India's Ranthambhor National Park.*
(Belinda Wright and Stanley Breeden)
Fifth frontispiece: *Tiger spoor in the mud of an Indian
wildlife preserve.* (Belinda Wright and Stanley Breeden)
Sixth frontispiece: *At sundown, five lionesses stalk a
distant antelope.* (Guenter Ziesler)

*Note on illustration numbers: All illustrations are numbered
according to the pages on which they appear.*

Contents

Introduction

Cedarville is a community of perhaps two hundred hardy souls on the sparsely populated eastern tip of Michigan's Upper Peninsula. The village takes its name from the forbidding, boggy forests of northern white-cedar that blanket this wild region on the north shore of Lake Huron. Far off the heavily traveled tourist routes, Cedarville gets few visitors except for sport fishermen and deer hunters. The cedar trees, cut for pulp, posts, and log cabins, are the main source of livelihood for residents who suffer swarms of mosquitoes and black flies in summer, bitter cold and deep snow in winter. It is not an especially memorable place.

Yet Cedarville, Michigan, found itself in the news on a regular basis in the winter of 1958 because of frequent sightings in the dead of night of a large, tawny, long-tailed beast bounding across a road from one cedar swamp to another. Travelers' descriptions invariably matched those of a mountain lion, or cougar—a carnivore last seen in the state in the 1800s. There are other wild cats in these tangled woods, but lynx and bobcats are short-tailed and one-tenth the size of *Felis concolor*. And deer with their flashing white tails and spindly legs would be hard to confuse with a low-slung cougar and its three-foot-long appendage. Mistaken identity seemed an unlikely explanation.

But lacking a corpus delicti, or other incontrovertible proof, biologists for the Michigan Game Division dismissed the sightings as the product of either vivid imagination or overimbibing of spirits. A mountain lion in Michigan, the experts said, was about as likely as a flying saucer ferrying little green men from Mars. Still, the credentials of some of the witnesses were impeccable: a state trooper, a deputy sheriff, a state legislator, a Catholic bishop!

At the time I was on the editorial staff of a small daily newspaper, and my dream was to become a famous writer of outdoor adventure stories like my hero Ben East, a fellow Michigander. I collected all the reports of mountain lion sightings near Cedarville, and sent off to *Outdoor Life* a story about the big cat's return to the North Country. It soon came back with a polite letter of rejection from Ben East himself, suggesting that his magazine didn't publish fiction. My hopes deflated, I burned the manuscript in embarrassment.

Still, I remain convinced that a cougar really was prowling those Michigan cedar swamps nearly three decades ago, feasting on deer, snowshoe hares, and porcupines, and making brief, startling appearances in the glare of motorists' headlights. I *want* to believe that there were and are cougars beyond the western mountains and Florida swamps, because their presence, however ephemeral, defies those who insist that the eastern United States has been totally tamed, its great predators exterminated long ago.

Like all wild felines, large and small, the cougar has suffered grievously at the hands of man, relentlessly trapped and poisoned as a killer of livestock and a predator on game animals. In India, thousands and thousands of Bengal tigers were wantonly killed for sport during the decades of British colonial rule; that the tiger still survives in modest numbers on the subcontinent is a small miracle. During the 1960s and early 1970s, the worldwide demand for expensive fur coats made from the skins of spotted cats threatened the leopard, cheetah, and jaguar with extinction, and brought intolerable pressure on smaller spotted cats like the ocelot and margay.

Strict enforcement of the federal Endangered Species Act and public scorn of anyone seen wearing a leopard or cheetah coat has put fur dealers in the United States out of the cat-skin business. Wildlife-protection laws in South America and Africa and an international treaty controlling traffic in rare animals have considerably slowed, but not halted altogether, the killing of big cats for the European market by professional poachers and natives. The leopard, for one, has begun to recover from its disastrously low ebb, and in many cases the loss of habitat and prey species is now of more immediate concern.

What worries conservationists most today is exploitation by the fashion trade—in place of the large, noble felines—of the world's thirty or so small cats. Among them are such familiar names as the bobcat, lynx, ocelot, and margay. A bobcat pelt, worth fifty cents not that long ago, now brings several hundred dollars at a fur auction. An ocelot coat costs $40,000 in West Germany, international hub of the legal and illicit trade in wild cat skins. But thousands of lesser-known species, such as Geoffroy's cat, the pampas cat, and the leopard cat, are also being killed for profit. Of the little spotted cat (*Felis tigrina*), one authoritative review of the world's mammals reports only this: "The little spotted cat lives in forests, and its habits in the wild are not known." That brief note could unfortunately become the little spotted cat's epitaph.

A world without wild cats—without cougars and tigers, leopards and lions, bobcats and ocelots, margays and jungle cats—would be an impoverished world indeed. Passing laws and ratifying treaties, however, will accomplish little without public support for both enforcement and habitat preservation. *The Audubon Society Book of Wild Cats*, a celebration of Earth's wondrous collection of unfettered felines, is our contribution to the educational process that one day may cause people everywhere to treasure these shy, brazen, lovely, and terrifying animals as part of our planet's heritage, rather than viewing them as a threat, a resource to be plundered, or an object of high fashion.

Les Line

16. *Crouched low to the ground, muscles tensed and ready to spring, a lioness (Panthera leo) warily watches a human intruder on Kenya's Masai Mara game reserve. Eight to nine feet long from nose to tail, an adult lioness will weigh from 270 to 400 pounds. A full-grown male lion is somewhat larger, although its mane gives it the appearance of much greater size. Among all of the world's felines, the lion is second in size to the tiger (Panthera tigris), but it is the legendary King of Beasts that has captured man's imagination for centuries.*

Lord of the Savannas

Welling out of the blackness, the roaring of lions seems to hush all the myriad cackles, hoots, snorts, and other sounds that enliven the African night. The primal music of the tawny cats begins with a series of deep, coughing grunts. Within moments, the grunts merge, then swiftly swell into a wild symphony that rolls over the landscape. To humans, the thunder of lions in the night evokes a primitive awe, harking back to a time more than two million years ago when our ancestors listened to the same noise and trembled.

The lion (*Panthera leo*) is the most distinctive of the big cats. Its color is primarily tawny, although it can be cast with gray or red. No other cat has a tuft at the end of its tail, a characteristic more marked in male than in female lions. Also unique among felines is the great ruff of a mane worn by many male lions; the mane, however, is lacking in females, who are much more slightly built than the males.

Among cats, the lion, at a maximum weight of 500 pounds, is second only to the tiger in size. Though its behavior is often far from regal, the lion alone has earned the title "King of Beasts," perhaps because few, if any, sounds in the animal kingdom are as frightening as the lion's roar, because a full-maned male lion simply looks royal, and because the lion is the top predator in a realm inhabited by huge beasts—the land of the wide-open, windswept savannas, thorn scrub, and desert fringes of Africa.

Contrary to what many people have been led to believe by films and comics, lions never frequent jungles or other deep forests. Their social behavior alone makes them unfit for big woods. Lions live in groups, called prides;

because lions are large, and because a pride may consist of many individuals, the cats can find sufficient food only in grasslands. These seas of grass provide enough nourishment to support the immense herds of horned and hoofed mammals needed to sustain lions; in forests, large mammals are few and far between.

The prides of lions that roam Africa's grasslands may consist of from three or four individuals to as many as a few dozen. Ostensibly, at least, the ruler of the pride is a male, often supported by one or two cohorts, also males, who share the responsibilities and fruits of dominance. But females and their young make up most of a pride; in actuality, a pride is a matriarchy because the lionesses are its core. They are usually related—mothers and daughters, sisters, nieces, and aunts—and remain with the pride for as as long as they and it exist. The males, on the other hand, are transitory. Scientists who followed a Serengeti lioness during her life span of fifteen years counted seven different dominant males who, with their companions, reigned temporarily over her pride. Some sets of dominant males seems to be unusually footloose and relinquish prides after remaining with them for only a year or two. Generally, however, the lord of the pride retains title as long as he can hold it against rivals. Strong and vital, the dominant male can fulfill his task of siring young and protecting his charges. As he ages, however, he is almost inevitably driven out or killed by a competitor.

Once driven from his throne, a deposed monarch wanders the plains alone, often bearing wounds from the battles over kingship. He may continue his lonely rovings for months or even years. Eventually, he creeps off to a solitary death.

The sight of a fallen ruler, spending his last hours alone in the grass, is haunting and solemn. Lying in the hot sun, wounds crusted and fur torn, he makes little effort to dismiss the flies that buzz about. Antelope and zebras graze nearby, unafraid, seeming to sense that his prowess has vanished. Now and then he may halfheartedly try to rise, but eventually he gives up, collapses, and almost serenely awaits the vultures and jackals that will be his last attendants.

As long as the dominant male rules, however, he takes stern measures to protect his throne. All young males are expelled from the pride when they are about three years old to prevent insurgency from within. The young bachelors, usually in groups of two or three, wander in almost aimless fashion until they can usurp a reigning monarch. Sometimes they may hang around the edges of a pride, relaxed but always watching for the approach of its ruler and his cohorts, who help him defend the pride in a fight.

The youngsters can spot the protectors of a pride from miles across the open savanna. Lying in the grass, the bachelor lions suddenly become alert, their ears up and eyes riveted on faraway specks that rapidly grow into full-size male lions. Confronted by the pride males, the bachelors usually give ground and fade into the grass. Struggles for overlordship are an important part of the complex social life of lions, the only cats that live in large groups. Each pride has its own territory, which is rigorously defended; roaring, in fact, seems to be a way of warning other lions away. The size of a territory varies according to conditions such as the abundance of game and the number of lions in a given place. A pride's territory can be twenty square miles or up to five times that area. Lions move through their territory seasonally, going to water spots, for example, during dry periods, but they rarely follow the game herds when their migrations take them beyond territorial boundaries. Instead, the prides wait for game to wander through their area.

Sometimes, when the boundaries of territories overlap, prides will wage war. Also, loss of the dominant male can spell disaster for a pride. Males from other prides may attack it, slaughtering the young and appropriating the females. Battles can be fought by either sex, but truly significant confrontations involve only the pride males. Clawing and biting, the huge cats often battle to the death. Some scientists speculate that the thickness of the male's mane may be an advantage in such frays because it shields the throat from an opponent's fangs.

Within the pride, things are generally peaceful. Lolling and lazing in the grass during the heat of day, a pride does not seem to have a care in the world. The males often doze by themselves, while females and young lions spread out in scattered knots, some cubs nursing, others playing in mock fights or draped over one another in slumbering heaps. The intimate physical contact that members of a pride have with one another—females, for instance, often rub muzzles in greeting—helps maintain bonds within the group.

Because of their tawny coats, the pride lounging in the brown scrub and grass can be all but invisible to an observer. At first, it may seem as if only a handful of lions are resting in the vegetation; in time, however, many others materialize out of the bush.

Most of a lion's day is spent indolently, but in early

morning and after dark the pride goes hunting. Predation is a family venture, with several lions, and often as many as half a dozen, converging on game. No other cat joins forces in such large numbers to hunt in this cooperative fashion.

Lions use various tactics in hunting. Sometimes they drive victims into ambush. Several of the cats may hide in the grass, while others rush a herd of prey and push them toward the lions under cover. Lions, most often lionesses, also use decoy tactics. Some members of the pride may remain clearly visible, attracting the attention of the game, while others sneak close enough to attempt a rush.

Lions prefer to creep as close as they can to their prey before they explode out of hiding in a final, thunderous rush. They try to strike their prey within seconds, for if a victim evades the charge, a lion has little chance of catching it a second time. The cat may chase its victim for fifty yards or more, occasionally hitting a top speed of forty miles an hour, but the lion is not built for a long pursuit, so it quickly gives up and begins to stalk another animal.

If it can seize its prey, the lion often tries to smother it by biting its snout and holding it shut. Or else the lion uses its powerful paws to pull back the victim's head and then bites the throat. Because they mostly take the weak, lions do not threaten herds but cull them instead. A single lion can eat more than forty pounds of meat in one sitting, but lions rarely feed every day, even if game is abundant. Estimates vary, but most scientists agree that on the average a single lion kills at least twenty large animals each year. Given that a lion may live thirty years, the cat may kill up to 600 animals.

Hunting as a sisterhood, lionesses can handle rugged big game, including the truculent and massive African buffalo—although when lions face an aroused buffalo herd, they quickly retreat. The cooperative hunting and killing of big game is advantageous because it makes it easier for the pride to feed its numerous members.

Cooperative hunting is also aided by the lion's breeding habits. Males usually mate with several females during the same period, which may last several days. Consequently, more than one female will have young of the same age, so some mothers can stay home in charge of the cubs while others go out to hunt. At mealtime, the strong males and females grab as much as they can, and the weak and cubs scrabble for leftovers. In lean times, many cubs starve. Yet because lions produce fairly large litters, the loss of young is not catastrophic. Furthermore, if a lioness's cubs die, she is ready to mate again in a very short time.

Lionesses are mature enough sexually to mate during their fourth year. When the female is ready to bear her young, she retreats from the hustle and bustle of pride life to a secluded corner—perhaps under a bush, in the rocks, or among a stand of trees. The nursery is shielded from bad weather and from wandering hyenas or leopards that might make a quick meal of helpless cubs. After a gestation period of about three and a half months, the cubs are born—blind, mewing, and covered with dark spots, which they lose in about a year. Almost immediately they begin nursing. The female has four nipples, although she may bear more than that number of young. In such cases, the chances are high that some of the cubs will quickly perish as they compete for food. The lowest number of young borne is usually two.

Lion cubs begin an all-meat diet at about four months of age, although they may begin to sample small bits of flesh two months before that. Because they live in open country, the cubs witness the hunting strategies of their mothers before they are weaned. Little by little, they accompany their parents on the hunt, tagging along behind as the adults stalk their prey.

By the time cubs are six months old they begin to participate in the hunt, if not in the kill. They assist the lionesses in driving game, using tooth and claw to haul a victim to earth. Not until they are well over a year old, however, can cubs kill by themselves, even though they seldom have to hunt on their own as long as they belong to a pride.

Recent research on lion prides in the bleak and sizzling Kalahari Desert of Botswana suggests that under adverse environmental conditions even the most stable of prides can disintegrate, although usually only temporarily. During drought, when water and game are scarce, members of the pride separate and spread out over vast distances. Hunting in ones and twos, they can no longer bring down large game, so they turn increasingly to smaller prey. Moreover, territorial boundaries break down and disputes are forgotten as game and water vanish. When the rains return, the pride members gradually return to their territories, form cohesive groups, and begin living socially once more. The limits of the territories are redefined, and life generally returns to normal. Again the lions take up the community life style that makes them unique among all of the felines.

It is a popular belief that lions are purely African.

Although they seem to be children of Africa in evolutionary terms, during the ages of prehistory the big cats spread north, east, and west and as far from their original home as Britain and India. During the ice ages, much of this area was virtually treeless, populated by the immense herds of game that lions need to survive. After the last glaciers turned to meltwater, however, forest advanced over the land, pushing the plains game and lions before it.

Even so, lions persisted for millennia in southern Europe and the Middle East. The Achaean Greeks whom Homer chronicled hunted them with long-bladed spears in the scrubby hills of their homeland, much as the tall Masai cattle herders of East Africa still do today despite the efforts of African governments to stop this traditional practice. Lions lingered in the wild and rugged country of the Balkans well into the period of classical Greece. Herodotus, famed historian of the fifth century B.C., wrote that lions abounded in Thrace during his time. And when the host of the Persian king Xerxes tramped through Thrace in 480 B.C. for a disastrous confrontation with the Greek city states, lions attacked and killed some of his baggage camels.

Mentioned 130 times in the Bible, lions belonging to the Asiatic race remained in Israel until the thirteenth century. Further east, they hung on for centuries in Iran. A British officer stationed in Iran wrote in 1876 that a "notorious" number of lions inhabited a valley near the city of Shiraz. The last cat in that valley was killed in 1923, and no lions have been seen anywhere in Iran since 1942. Until the fall of Shah Mohammad Reza Pahlavi, the Iranian government planned to import a few Asiatic lions from India's Gir National Park, a region of thorn scrub and grazing land in the state of Gujarat, where the last wild prides of this critically endangered species survive. The Iranians hoped to release the lions in a few remote preserves in the center of their country. Since the revolution, however, the plan has been abandoned.

Asiatic lions, however, have returned to Israel—via San Diego, California. About seventy-five pairs of these rare cats exist in American and European zoos, where they are the subjects of intensive captive-breeding programs. The San Diego Zoo's Wild Animal Park has been especially successful with Asiatic lions, and more than a dozen cubs have been born there. During the summer of 1984, four cubs—two males and two females—were sent from San Diego to the wildlife reserve Hai Bar in Israel's Negev Desert. The reserve was created in 1969 to preserve wildlife that was native to the area in Biblical times. The lions at Hai Bar live in a fenced-in predator center, not freely as do the ibex and antelope that inhabit the rest of the reserve.

Even in Gir National Park, located near India's west coast, the lions lack the freedom to wander far and wide. About 200 of the creatures range the 500 square miles of the park and 200 square miles surrounding it. Although they are not fenced in, they are virtually prisoners because the area is almost completely surrounded by densely populated agricultural land. Agriculture, moreover, is closing in increasingly on the lion's range, and, say scientists who have studied the lions, it is the greatest threat to their existence.

Much of the Gir also is overgrazed by the cattle and buffalo herders, called maldharis, who traditionally have lived in the area and are allowed to stay in the park. Some conservationists have argued for the removal of the maldharis and their livestock, but others contend that the livestock, especially cattle, are essential to the survival of the lions because these domestic ungulates furnish about three quarters of the cats' food. Wild prey such as the nilgai antelope and the sambar deer is rare in the park, while approximately 40,000 cattle and buffalo graze there.

About half the cows and buffalo killed by lions do not end up as food for the big cats. Not as aggressive toward humans as their African relatives, the lions of the Gir are easily chased from their kills by the maldharis. Male lions simply go on to make another kill, but females with cubs in tow are not as mobile and often go hungry once they are driven from downed prey. As a result, many cubs starve to death, making the lions' situation even more precarious.

The maldharis receive some compensation from the government for lost livestock, but it is small and often not forthcoming at all. Some conservationists suggest that if better compensated, the herdsmen would maintain their cattle in the park and leave the kills for the lions. This prediction remains to be proven, but unquestionably the survival of the last wild Asiatic lions depends on achieving a balance between them, the livestock, the maldharis, and the land on which they all live.

Although still primarily hunters of wild game, Africa's lions face a future of increased involvement with humans. Approximately 200,000 lions rove Africa's plains and savannas, living for the most part as their primal ancestors did. But they have vanished from the extreme north and south of the continent and from other vast regions where they once hunted. Again, the cats have given ground to agriculture and grazing, and significant numbers of lions remain only in remote areas, national parks, and reserves.

One of the remaining strongholds of Africa's lions is the immense Serengeti-Mara ecosystem, a great mosaic of grassland and scattered woodland sprawling over 9,600 square miles of southwestern Kenya and northwestern Tanzania. The lions of this spectacular wilderness gorge on the colossal herds of animals that graze there—one and a half million wildebeests, a half million Thomson's gazelles, a quarter million common zebras, plus myriad elands, hartebeests, waterbuck, impalas, and more.

The lions of the Serengeti-Mara have been studied by scientists more thoroughly than those of any other area. Some prides have been observed continuously for years, with generations charted as they were born, grew, matured, and died. Much of what scientists know about the life of the lion in the wild comes from observations made in the Serengeti-Mara.

Even the Serengeti-Mara, however, is experiencing ecological pressures, which threaten not only its great herds of ungulates but also the lions and other predators that feed about them. In many areas, such as along the Kenya-Tanzania border, the populations of pastoralists—chiefly the Masai people—are mushrooming. The herders and their cattle and goats are encroaching on the great preserve. Not only do livestock compete with wild grazers for food, but occasionally they spread the dread bovine disease, rindepest. A rindepest epidemic could wreak havoc among the Serengeti-Mara herds. And if the numbers of ungulates drops, so will those of lions.

In Tanzania, economic problems that beset the government also are endangering the Serengeti-Mara. The once-efficient Tanzania national parks system is in disarray. Park rangers lack vehicles and other equipment needed to combat poaching, and ecological management of the ecosystem has declined. Conservationists in the United States and Europe, however, are mounting campaigns to assist Kenya and Tanzania in protecting and managing the Serengeti-Mara. With assistance, the African governments involved should be able to preserve this vast area of wilderness, and the sound of lions in the night will continue to thunder over the savannas.

25. *Grassland, savanna, woodland, even desert—all are suitable habitats for the African lion. Indeed, this black-maned lion from the Kalahari Desert in southern Africa inhabits a region where rain may not fall for months at a time and moisture-filled melons help quench the big cat's thirst. Dense forest, however, is inhospitable to lions, for large prey is scarce and the thick vegetation hinders hunting in groups.*

26 *overleaf. Young male lions sport a modest ruff, but their full, glorious manes appear in a burst of growth when they reach sexual maturity at the age of about four years. Strutting before a lioness, the King of Beasts cuts an impressive figure. The mane is often much darker than the tawny yellow coat that blends so well with the dry grassland. The Cape lion from the southern tip of Africa, extinct since 1865, is considered a subspecies,* Panthera leo malanochaitus, *because of its lush, black mane. Male lions without manes and lionesses with small manes occur on occasion.*

28 *overleaf. A lioness sprawls on her back in front of an attentive male. Within moments she will rise and travel a short distance, with the male eagerly following her until she signals that she is ready to mate. Male lions are polygamous, mating throughout the year with the different females within their pride.*

30 and **31.** *In the lion's world, mating is a frequent, fast, and rough-and-tumble affair. A pair of lions will separate from the pride, copulating several times a day, the male nipping the neck of the lioness as he mounts her, then leaping off in a hurry to avoid her bared teeth.*

32 and **33.** With a final roar of passion, lion and lioness roll apart, then nap to recover from their brief but violent union. Male lions in a pride seldom hunt—they are not as agile as lionesses and their manes are too conspicuous— but they provide more than mating service to the group. By spraying, scraping, and roaring, they define the pride's territory, which may encompass 150 square miles.

34. *Resting after copulation, a lioness sleeps while her mate strikes a contented, regal pose. Peaceful moments like this one are common within a pride. Throughout the day, adult males loll drowsily on the grass while females and young alternately sleep and play.*

36 *overleaf. Weighing three pounds at birth, lion cubs have woolly brown fur covered with spots and stripes, particularly on the forehead, and gray eyes that will turn the normal amber color in about three months.*

35. *Later in the day, as a thunderstorm threatens, the male and female move slowly back to their pride. Their pairing will produce a litter of two or three cubs after a gestation period of 105 to 108 days. Born in a secluded nursery, the cubs will be introduced to the pride when they are four to six weeks old.*

38 and **39.** *All of the lionesses in a pride have litters at about the same time, and cubs will nurse at the nipples of any available female, not just their mother.*

40 *overleaf. Roaring in feigned outrage, a male lion tolerates a nip on the rump from a playful cub. Males will stand guard over the pride's new generation while the lionesses hunt, for the cubs are in constant danger of being killed by nomadic lions or males from neighboring prides.*

42 and **43.** *For lion cubs, the growing-up process is a long one. It takes a young lion three years to acquire the hunting skills necessary to participate as a full member of the pride or to survive on its own in the wild over a life span of ten to twelve years. And so there is plenty of time for rambunctious play with siblings and cousins. By the age of fifteen months a cub will weigh 100 pounds, have permanent teeth, and be able to compete for its share of a kill. Females will remain with the pride and breed in their fourth year; newly adult males leave for a bachelor life or join other prides.*

44 *overleaf. A young male lion drives two lionesses away from a kill, which he will share with the pride's small cubs. Except for such brief spats over food, life in the clan is harmonious and cooperative, and a lion that is seriously injured in the hunt stands a far better chance of survival than a solitary leopard that must fend for itself.*

46 and **47.** *Class is assembled in the sere grass of the Masai Mara as several half-grown lion cubs watch the pride's lionesses stalk a herd of wildebeests. By accompanying adults on the hunt, and no doubt bungling their first attempts at a kill, the fast-growing youngsters learn how to hunt in a group, to stalk downwind, and to fell prey as large and dangerous as buffalo.*

48 *and* **49; 50** *overleaf. Stalking to within fifty yards of a wildebeest, a lioness attacks in a final, deadly rush. Sinking its claws into the rump, the big cat drags its victim to the ground, then holds it with a strangling grip on the throat while other lions hurry over to feed. The wildebeest likely will die from evisceration. Wildebeests are migratory, and nomadic lions follow them on their endless quest for grazing lands. When the ungulates move beyond the pride's territory, the resident lions face lean hunting, being compelled to rely on such difficult prey as buffalo, topi, and impala. When food is scarce, cubs often perish of starvation.*

52 and **53**. *Midafternoon finds a lion pride slumbering in the thin, dappled shade of a thorntree. Like housecats, lions sleep away much of their lives and are active only four or five hours a day. They often hunt in broad daylight, but on the African plains where cover is scant, nocturnal stalks have a greater chance of success.*

54 *overleaf. An alert lioness at sunrise on the Masai Mara. Six animals—zebra, wildebeest, hartebeest, topi, buffalo, and warthog—account for most of the lion's food supply. But the prey of the King of Beasts ranges from young elephants and rhinoceroses to baboons, birds, fish, and even crocodiles!*

56. *Mountain lion, cougar, puma, panther—the American lion (Felis concolor) is a cat of numerous vernacular names. Those are the ones most commonly used, not only by the laity but by experts as well, for even scientists are unable to agree on a common term. But there are other, more colorful names, like painter (favored by the mountain men and fur trappers of the 1800s, who preferred lion to all other wild meat), catamount, mountain screamer, Indian devil, and silver lion. The beast that owns all these handles may stretch 8 feet long, a third of that length accounted for by its flowing tail.*

The American Lion

Anxious to reach home, a motorist steers his car along a country road in northwestern Connecticut, about 100 miles from Manhattan. It is close to midnight, and because he is tired he watches the road carefully. As the car rounds a bend, an astonishing sight appears, momentarily bathed in the glare of his headlights before it vanishes into the trees. The driver halts, not believing what he has just seen: a large, tawny animal with a low, sinuous body and a tail almost a yard long that is carried in a graceful droop. The motorist has glimpsed the second-largest feline in the New World, a cat of many names—the mountain lion (*Felis concolor*), the lion of the Americas, the cougar.

During the 1950s and 1960s, an increasing number of people in the northeastern United States reported sighting this large cat, which was long thought to have vanished from the region. First discounted by scientists, some of the reports finally were verified. Biologists now know that the "mountain lion"—actually not a true lion nor restricted to mountains—roves parts of the Northeast, mostly in and around the Appalachians.

The survival of the mountain lion in the northeastern United States demonstrates the remarkable adaptability of this cat. Among felines, only the leopard can boast a similar ability to survive under such a wide range of ecological and geographical conditions, even including proximity to urban centers.

When Europeans arrived in the Americas, the mountain lion was distributed over more territory than any other land mammal in the Western Hemisphere. This lithe cat prowled across the continents from northern Canada to the southern tip of South America. Over this vast range

the creature was given many names: cougar, puma, panther, catamount, painter—more than forty in English and about five dozen in Spanish and Indian tongues.
In North America today, however, cougars are abundant only from the Rocky Mountains to the Pacific Coast. They have vanished from the central United States and are rare in the East. Small numbers of cougars rove Florida, and perhaps a few dozen inhabit the Appalachians from the Canadian Maritime Provinces to Georgia, although the population seems to be slowly increasing. South of Texas, cougars are scattered over wide areas, in numbers that are uncertain. Although they have been exterminated in many regions, the cats are still common in parts of Mexico and Central America, as well as scattered throughout South America, especially in the wild reaches of Patagonia, which is one of their most secure havens.
An examination of some of the places where cougars live testifies to their ecological adaptability. They hunt the watery wilderness of Florida's Everglades and the sun-scorched Sonoran Desert. The snowy peaks of the Rockies and the Andes echo from their chilling screams. Cougars haunt the soggy jungles of Central America and the bone-dry wastes of Baja California. They are notably common in British Columbia, especially on Vancouver Island, where they are seen regularly despite their elusive nature. These tawny cats even make their homes in and around some large cities located near extensive tracts of wilderness.
Despite occasional excursions to populated areas, cougars are true loners, so elusive they have been called ghosts of the wilderness. Except when adults are driven by the urge to mate, they avoid even their own kind. A cougar does not need a first-hand encounter to know if another cougar is nearby because these cats leave signs of their presence: they scratch deeply into the soil, often as much as a half foot below the surface, then urinate on the spot.
Cougars regularly leave such scrapes within their territories, which are about twenty square miles per adult. The spots chosen by the cats for scrapes are often where their trails cross, beneath trees, or on high spots such as ridges. Normally, when a wandering cougar comes upon the scrape of another it will change course. By avoiding one another, cougars are able to maintain their personal territories without fighting. An animal that lives on its own would not survive long if continually injured in territorial battles.
Although they alert their fellow cats that they are in the

vicinity, cougars are masters at avoiding humans. Many people who have lived in cougar country all their lives have never spied one of the creatures. Most often, the only evidence cougars give of their presence are their tracks, their scat, or, less commonly, their spine-chilling yowl, which is sometimes likened to the scream of a terrified woman. The covertness of the cougar is one of the keys to its adaptability, because it is able to go unnoticed by humans, unless it takes to activities such as stock killing. Few, if any, other big cats are as unobtrusive.

Although the cougar is termed a "big cat," the typical cougar is less than half the weight of the average lion. A large cougar can reach a weight of more than 275 pounds and a length of more than nine feet from its snout to the tip of its tail. Most, however, are much smaller, although well over 100 pounds.

The cougar's dietary versatility is another proof of its remarkable adaptability. South American cougars stalk guanacos, wild relatives of the domestic llama. The intrepid cats climb the crags of the Rockies to prey upon mountain goats and bighorn sheep, no easy adversaries. When need be, the cougar eats insects, fish, rodents, and small mammals, including porcupines and beavers. The mainstay of the cougar's diet, however, is deer.

Several species of deer live within the cougar's vast range. In South America these include the diminutive pudus of the Andes and the hefty swamp deer that feed in marshy savannas and soggy forests from the Guianas to Uruguay. Cougars in western North America sometimes kill elk and moose, although mostly weak, old individuals or calves. From the Great Plains to the Pacific, mule deer furnish part of the cougar's diet. Throughout North America, however, the most important deer in terms of the cougar's survival is the whitetail. With the exception of the Pacific Coast and the Great Basin, the original range of the cougar coincided with that of the whitetail. Where the whitetail thrived, so did the cougar. Biologists suspect, in fact, that the resurgence of the cougar in eastern North America is linked to the explosion of the whitetail population there. Cougars often travel for long distances in search of prey, within any given day roving for almost a score of miles. Of course, the distance a cougar travels is largely determined by the availability of game. If the immediate vicinity is teeming with prey, the cat does not need to venture as far to fill its belly. Females with young in the den, moreover, cannot travel far without leaving their cubs unprotected.

Family life for cougars is mostly restricted to mother and young. Males—like their smaller tomcat kin—mate with whatever females are available. Cougars seem to mate at almost any time of year, no matter where they live. Once a male and female cougar link up they stay together no longer than a few weeks, often less.

Almost three months after mating, a cougar usually has two or three young, but on occasion five or six may be born. However, it is difficult for a female to care for a large number of cubs; therefore, an unusually large litter is usually reduced through natural attrition.

Few felines are as fetching as infant cougars. They sport rings on their tails and dark spots on their tawny coats, but these markings disappear within a few months. Young cougars weigh a pound or less at birth but grow to more than thirty pounds by six months of age. Blind for their first two weeks of life, they live exclusively on mother's milk for a month, after which their parent begins to provide them with tidbits of flesh. Even so, the young may continue living partly on milk for another four or five months.

Occasionally, orphaned cougars are reared by people who work for conservation groups or zoos. In a household a cub can be totally entertaining, yet it always provides evidence that it is, in the end, not a pet but a wild animal. To the knowledgeable human eye, what appears to be play is really practice for the wilderness life it will lead as it matures. Rough-and-tumble play and the stalking of butterflies, wind-blown leaves, or anything else that moves function as preludes to the hunting and killing that is the way of the adult cougar.

One small orphaned cougar, about two months old and the size of a house cat, used to stalk the four-year-old son of its human foster parents. Lying on a couch, the cat would leap upon the youngster—who enjoyed the activity—push him to the rug, and nip the child on the nape of the neck with teeth that could not cause any damage. The routine was almost a replica of that used by adults to kill deer.

In the wild cubs are weaned at about five months, then roam the woods with their mother, killing prey as they move along. The mother and cubs often remain together for a year, sometimes even a few months more, before they separate. After that, they go their distant ways. Like their mother, the young become wilderness wraiths with the ability to survive—at least partially—in environments altered by humans.

61. *Historically, the mountain lion stalked its prey across North and South America. Today, north of the Mexican border, its primary range has shrunk to the wilderness areas of the West, from British Columbia and Alberta to California and Texas. An endangered population of "panthers" manages to hang on in the trackless swamps of Florida. And the most heartening news for fans of the mountain lion is the increasing number of sightings from New England to the Appalachians, suggesting that this tawny predator may one day reinhabit the eastern forests from which it was chased by the end of the nineteenth century.*

62 *overleaf. When fully grown, this young male mountain lion will weigh as much as 225 pounds. His mate will be much smaller: The average female cougar weighs only 100 pounds and is less than 6 feet long, including its tail. To early explorers from Europe, the American feline's uniformly colored coat suggested the African lion, the only other big cat with fur of a solid color. The mountain lion, of course, has no mane. Its coat varies from rufous to tawny to gray, and on very rare occasions a "black panther" with melanistic hues will be sighted, most often in the Florida Everglades.*

64 *right. A mountain lion cub will remain with its mother for two years before striking out in search of a home range it can claim as its own. The life span of a mountain lion, which has no enemies except man, is estimated at fifteen to eighteen years.*

64 *above. Bounding through the snow of the Rockies, all four feet landing close together, a mountain lion can clear 30 feet or even 40 feet in a single leap. The front paws of a mountain lion will leave a round print that is 3¼ to 4 inches long. The cat's head is small for the size of its body, and this, together with those long legs, suggests a distant link to the cheetah. For a short distance a mountain lion can outrun a deer, the animal on which the cat most often preys. But usually it stalks to within a pounce or two of its victim, then leaps on its back, knocking the deer to the ground while sinking its teeth and claws into the neck and shoulders.*

66 *and* **68** *overleaves. The mountain lion is a solitary hunter except during the brief mating period, when for two weeks male and female prowl the forests side by side. A male mountain lion maintains a home range that, in winter, will cover up to 30 square miles, marking the boundaries by scraping pine needles and dirt into piles on which the cat urinates and leaves its feces. Unlike other big felines—the African lion, tiger, leopard, and jaguar—the mountain lion cannot roar. Silent most of the year, it rends the wilderness night with blood-curdling screams at mating time.*

70 *right. Although this mountain lion has dispatched a rattlesnake with disregard for its lethal venom, attacks on large animals are not without risk. Elk, in particular, have been known to inflict fatal injuries on their feline tormentors. Often a cougar will fall from the back of its target, resulting in a broken nose or a cracked skull.*

70 *top two rows and* **72** *overleaf. A mountain lion races across a mountain meadow in pursuit of a deer. Eight out of every ten attacks on deer by a mountain lion are successful, one researcher estimates, and where deer are abundant, the cat will take an average of one animal every week. Other large prey includes elk, moose, bighorn sheep, pronghorns —and, to the dismay of ranchers, sheep, cattle, and horses. But mountain lions also hunt beaver, skunks, coyotes, marmots, hares, mice, birds, grasshoppers, and even porcupines. In Central and South America, peccaries and such large rodents as pacas and agoutis are common prey of* Felis concolor.

74 *overleaf. On a hot summer day, a mountain lion cools off in a shallow stream. Misunderstood by sportsmen unwilling to share the deer and elk herds with a natural predator, and hated by ranchers for its raids on livestock,* Felis concolor *has been persecuted for more than two centuries. In 1764 Massachusetts offered a bounty of four English pounds for a "panther" scalp. In one county in Pennsylvania, 600 cougars were killed between 1820 and 1845. The last record of a mountain lion in that state—until recent years— was in 1891.*

76. *In North America, the lynx* (Felis lynx) *is found only in northern forests that are snowbound for several months each year. Boreal forests are the primary haunt of the lynx in Eurasia as well, but in the Old World it ranges far to the south into what would seem to be unlikely habitats: Lynx, for instance, prowl the sand dunes and pine-oak scrublands of the Coto de Doñana preserve in southern Spain. The face of the lynx is startling: Its ears have long black tufts, and large cheek ruffs form a double-pointed beard.*

Prowlers of the North

Venturing forth from a grove of conifers, a red fox cocks its ears and listens for the sound of mice below the snow. Food has been scarce during the grim northern winter, and the fox is desperately hungry. So, however, is another predator of the boreal forest. Keen yellow eyes watch the fox as it moves from the cover of the trees into deeper snow. The fox is in mortal danger, for the snow has impeded the nimbleness that in another season would help it escape from the lynx (*Felis lynx*) that stalks it, ever so stealthily, belly to the ground.

Like a steel spring uncoiled, the lynx hurtles toward the fox with an explosive, fluid leap. Although the fox manages to twist its body away from the cat's grasping claws, it is still doomed. It tries to run but founders in the drifts. The lynx, on the other hand, bounds easily over the surface after its prey. Even though twice the weight of the fox, the cat does not sink; its oversize feet, heavily padded with hair, support it in the snow.

The lynx's snowshoe feet mark it as an animal of the northland—the forests that stretch from temperate latitudes to the southern fringes of the Arctic. Almost everywhere that the lynx lives, snow covers the ground for several months a year. Only along Europe's Mediterranean rim, the southern margins of the lynx's range, does it inhabit a region where winters are relatively mild—and there it roves mountainous regions with climates similar to those of more northern latitudes. In North America, the bobcat (*Felis rufus*), which closely resembles the lynx, replaces it at latitudes and altitudes too warm to support boreal forest. The bobcat ranges from the Canadian border country into Mexico but is absent from parts of the central Midwest and

Southeast. More adaptable than the lynx, the bobcat fares well in a variety of habitats, including deep forests, deserts, swamps, and scrub. Although it roams sun-soaked lands edging the tropics, the bobcat is basically a creature of north-temperate latitudes.

Although bobcats are creatures of the wild, they can and do live in places where human populations are relatively dense, such as southern New England. Bobcats even venture into some cities—Washington, D.C., for example—entering via natural conduits, such as brushy and forested river valleys. Human residents of bobcat country seldom see them, however, because these animals are almost exclusively nocturnal and are extremely stealthy. The lynx is also a nocturnal creature, except in the Arctic, where the long summer days force the cat to seek its food in sunlight.

Both bobcats and lynx are good-size cats, weighing from about eleven to fifteen pounds and reaching approximately two feet at the shoulder. The body of the lynx is somewhat more compact than that of the bobcat. A big lynx can measure slightly less than four feet in length, while the largest bobcats are just over four feet. Bobcats and lynx are loners, males and females going their own way except during the late winter, when the urge to reproduce draws them to enthusiastic, if hasty, mating. In his quest for a mate, the male bobcat is anything but secretive. He yowls like a banshee in the darkness, as if to tell other males to keep clear while he announces his presence to females in the vicinity—and sometimes scaring the wits out of people who hear the spine-chilling racket.

Female lynx have up to four kittens per litter; bobcats, usually three. At birth, the kittens are tiny, weighing less than a pound each. Their home is usually a hollow log or a dry cavity under the roots of a tree. Kittens are weaned in about two months and then begin to hunt with their mother. This is the only time when these cats socialize with others of their kind for a relatively long period. Young bobcats remain with their parent until autumn, when, half-grown in size, they set out on their own. Lynx usually follow the same pattern, but occasionally the young remain with their mother all winter, hunting prey together.

Because bobcats and lynx are unable to run fast for long distances, they stalk and ambush their prey. Belly close to the ground, the cats creep as close as they can and then burst out of the shadowy brush to pounce upon their victims. The cats also like to drop on prey from low-hanging tree limbs or ledges.

Bobcats sometimes cover more than twenty miles patrolling the countryside for food. On the hunt, a bobcat investigates fallen trees, crevices, brushy tangles— almost anywhere a victim might be hiding. The cat is not particular about its prey. It feeds on rabbits, hares, ground birds, mice, and even wild turkeys, occasionally killing deer, especially fawns, old or sick animals, or ones bogged down in heavy snow and unable to flee. The bobcat's varied diet is one of the reasons it can live in so many different habitats.

The bobcat shares some of its versatility and adaptability with the lynx of Eurasia. Some scientists have recognized the Eurasian lynx as a species distinct from that of North America. Although the Eurasian lynx is primarily a cat of the forests, unlike its North American cousin, it ranges widely through hardwoods as well as coniferous woodlands. Eurasian lynxes, moreover, inhabit some open country, such as the mosaic of sand dunes, pink and oak scrub, and marshes in Spain's Coto de Doñana delta of the Guadalquivir River. They also prowl the grassy upland meadows of Iran's towering Alborz Mountains south of the Caspian Sea and the barren Tibetan Plateau.

Like bobcats, Eurasian lynxes also have a more cosmopolitan diet than North American lynx. Red deer, roe deer, reindeer, ibex, wild sheep, ground birds, wild boar, pigeons, marmots, rabbits, and hares all furnish sustenance for Old World lynx. North American lynx prey on rodents, birds, and deer. Yet one species is critical to their survival—the snowshoe hare, a creature that, like the lynx, has broad, hairy feet adapted for traveling in deep snow.

The number of lynx and hares fluctuates in a precise interaction that vividly dramatizes how populations of prey and predator affect each other. The number of hares varies cyclically, peaking about every ten years. When the cycle is reaching its zenith, lynx prosper, literally surrounded by food; within only a square mile of territory, a single cat may find all the hares it needs to keep fat and healthy.

After peaking, however, the numbers of hares decline. So do the numbers of lynx, although the cat population starts to decline up to a year after the hares have begun to die out. As the hares reach their nadir, life turns harsh for the lynx. They must range far and wide for food, in some instances traveling hundreds of miles. Prey that the cats snubbed in good times, such as foxes, become the edge between them and starvation. And in the end, many lynx do starve; the population of lynx in a given area may drop to less than ten percent of its maximum.

Fewer lynx, however, means decreased predation upon the hares. Gradually their numbers begin to build again, and, subsequently, so do those of the lynx. The endless round keeps prey and predator in balance as long as humans do not interfere.

Human interference is usually directed at predators. The lynx has declined throughout its circumpolar range because its habitat has been altered and because, given the chance, it will prey on domestic animals such as sheep and goats. The pressure on the lynx has been greatest in Europe, where since the turn of the century the creature's range has been drastically reduced. Once widespread in Western Europe, the lynx has been pushed into inaccessible refuges, such as the mountains of northern Scandinavia, the Transylvanian Alps of Rumania, the rugged Tatry Mountains on the Polish-Czechoslovak border, the backwaters of the Balkans, and remote areas of southern Spain. The Spanish, or pardel, lynx (*Felis lynx pardina*) is thought by some biologists to be an entirely different species. It is slightly smaller than the lynx of Europe and North America and its coat is more heavily spotted.

Lynx are more abundant in the deep forests of the Soviet Union and eastern Asia. Moreover, in at least one area, the Slovenian Republic of Yugoslavia, the cat has been reintroduced with successful results. The lynx disappeared from the Slovenian countryside toward the end of the nineteenth century. During the 1970s, Slovenian conservationists obtained three pairs of the cats from Czechoslovakia and freed them in mountain wilderness that still characterizes much of the northern Yugoslav republic. Within less than a decade, lynx numbers there had increased to more than a hundred cats, with all signs pointing to a continued expansion of the population.

The North American lynx similarly has been pushed from parts of its traditional range, although not only because of human activity. When Europeans first arrived in the New World, the lynx lived as far south as the Middle Atlantic states. It retreated north as forests were cleared but also, biologists suspect, because winters moderated. The bobcat, meanwhile, seems to have edged north into Canada beyond its former range and has vanished from much of the lands it previously inhabited. Even so, with sound conservation management, the bobcat should continue to prowl through North America's countryside for many years to come.

81. *Named for its stubby tail, the bobcat (Felis rufus) is found only in North America, from southernmost Canada to Florida, Texas, and Mexico. The bobcat's territory begins where that of the lynx leaves off, and the two cats are seldom encountered in the same area—even if the habitat is perfect for the lynx and food supplies are substantial. The reason, scientists say, is the more aggressive nature of the bobcat, which has to compete with coyotes and cougars to survive. They note that Canada's 4,000-square-mile Cape Breton Island was lynx country exclusively until it was linked to Nova Scotia by a causeway in the 1950s. In three decades, bobcats have pushed the lynx from much of the island.*

82 *overleaf. This half-grown bobcat kitten will soon leave its mother's side. Bobcat kittens are born in early spring in a hollow log or a dry den beneath the roots of a fallen tree, usually in litters of three. They weigh less than a pound at birth, open their eyes in nine days, are weaned at two months, and hunt with their parent until autumn. Except for the briefest of mating periods in late winter, the male bobcat leads a solitary life year-round. Its quest for a female is announced with yowls and screams that will raise the hackles of man or beast.*

84 and **85.** *The bobcat is a skilled climber, and it will use a tree as a resting place, a scratching post to sharpen its claws and limber its muscles, or—if surprised with a freshly killed cottontail rabbit—a temporary refuge from an intruder. Occasionally a bobcat will rob a woodpecker nest, but normally it hunts on the ground, locating prey by sight, not scent. Rabbits and hares, squirrels and mice top the list, which also includes marmots, porcupines, muskrats, grouse, and even bats, turtles, and fish.*

86 *overleaf. With the gift of extraordinary night vision, the lynx waits for darkness to begin its hunt. If prey is abundant, it may lie in wait on a boulder or limb overlooking a well-used game trail. Or it will stalk the dense coniferous forest, crouched low to the ground, creeping to within a few feet of an intended victim before making its deadly leap. Mammalogist Victor Cahalane describes this moment of truth in dramatic terms: "Its nose twitches, muscles tighten, ears are laid back, and the hard yellow eyes measure the distance and actions of the prey. Then, like steel springs, its muscles send it flying through the air."*

90 *overleaf. A heavily spotted coat and slightly smaller size set the Spanish lynx apart from its relatives in northern Europe. Some biologists, in fact, consider it a separate species and give it the name pardel lynx* (Felis lynx pardina). *In much of Europe, the lynx has retreated under pressure from civilization to remote mountain refuges. Conservationists, however, have reintroduced the cat into Yugoslavia with great success.*

88 *and* 89. *Few wild hunters are as much at home in deep snow as the lynx. Like snowshoes, its large, thickly furred feet enable it to walk atop the lightest crust, and it will sink only an inch or two in freshly fallen snow. A soft coat of hairs four inches long keeps the lynx warm in the deep-freeze of the subarctic. Like the bobcat, the lynx prefers a solitary life, but the young remain with their mother through their first winter, and two or more lynx families may hunt together, spreading out in military fashion as they search the white-clad forest.*

92 *and* **93**; **94** *overleaf. In North America, the lynx preys largely on snowshoe hares, and the predator's numbers are directly tied to the abundance of its prey. Hare populations are cyclical, and when they reach their zenith—about every ten years—a female lynx will produce as many as six young per year with little mortality among the kittens. But as the supply of hares declines, the lynx population also crashes. In times of hunger, a lynx may be driven to attack deer, caribou, or wild sheep several times its size, but unless the hooved animal is weakened by winter starvation or illness, the effort is certain to fail and may result in serious injuries to the cat.*

96. *Ancestor of the domestic cat, the Old World wildcat (Felis silvestris) looks much like a domestic tabby. Its long, gray fur is broken by dark vertical stripes; its tail is ringed and ends in a blunt black tip. It is more muscular than its pampered relatives, but so close is the link that wildcats readily mate with household pets turned feral. The wildcat's original range reached from the British Isles and Scandinavia to Africa and to the Middle East, where it was first domesticated 7,000 years ago. Over the centuries more than thirty breeds have evolved from those first tamed tabbies.*

Tabby's Relatives

At the turn of the century, British archaeologists probing the ruins of ancient Egyptian tombs discovered thousands of mummified cats—so many, in fact, that tons of the feline remains were shipped back to England for processing into fertilizer. Scientists who examined the mummies found two species, the African wildcat (*Felis libyca*) and the jungle cat (*Felis chaus*), which the Egyptians apparently kept as pets and mousers. These species, found today in much of the Old World, seem to be the ancestors of the domestic cat. In overall appearance, the wildcat especially resembles a tabby—the blotched or striped cat familiar to modern-day pet owners—the links between the animals being substantiated by the facts that the two readily interbreed and that many domestic cats in Africa have wildcat blood. The wildcats and the domestic cat have about the same dimensions, although the wildcat is more powerfully built and has longer legs than its tame relative. The long legs of the wildcat give it a more graceful, fluid appearance than the tabby. Some observers have claimed that the long-legged gait of the wildcat has more in common with the stride of the cheetah than of domestic felines. All in all, the wildcat is a more formidable animal than the tabby, although feral housecats can act almost as fierce as their wild kin. The wildcat and the jungle cat are among a handful of similar species that range much of the Old World, from northern Europe to the swamps of the tropics. Of these, the wildcat covers the greatest geographical area and copes with the widest variety of environmental conditions. The original range of the wildcat was vast, from the British Isles through the Middle East and to southern Africa. Wildcats are primarily woodland creatures but shun deep jungle, so they are absent from the great rain forest that forms a sea of green across the central and western parts of Africa's midsection.

Because wildcats are primarily forest or bush animals, they are not at home in deserts—they do not live in the Sahara or the Kalahari, for instance—but they can survive in country that is relatively dry and open as long as scattered trees grow there. These cats are common, for example, in the grassy mountain valleys of northern Iran, a wild landscape towering over the southern margin of the Caspian seashore that is so open, the creatures are known locally as "steppe cats."

Throughout its considerable range, the wildcat has evolved into many different species that generally look alike but may vary in color. Some are reddish brown or gray, like the European cat. All bear dark transverse stripes, with another stripe running down the spine, and the tail is darkly ringed and tipped with black. Some scientists believe that the Asian and African wildcats differ from the European species, but scientists tend to classify them as one.

Today, wildcats have vanished from much of their range in Europe and the Middle East due to the destruction of forests and their persecution as predators. The forests of beech, maple, oaks, and spruce in the Caucasus, however, are sufficiently rugged and remote for wildcats to survive there. A few even hide out in the mountains of Syria, where patches of woodland have not been cut or eaten away by goats and sheep.

The European version of the wildcat originally inhabited most of the continent from the British Isles to the fringes of Asia, but it now exists mostly in scattered, inaccessible pockets. The last refuge of the wildcat in the British Isles is Scotland's windswept Highlands, particularly the ancient Grampian hills, which are rocky and covered with moors. The forests of Bavaria support a few wildcats, as do the mountains of eastern Europe. Another of the cat's havens is the rugged hills and mountains that rim the northern shores of the Mediterranean from Spain to Turkey. There, and on islands such as Corsica and Sardinia, the wildcat lurks in the dense, tangled recesses of a scrubby woodland called maquis, or *macchia*. An Old World counterpart of the chaparral of Mexico and the southwestern United States, maquis is a combination of stunted and gnarled oaks, low pines, heaths, and brambles that hold tenaciously to rocky, eroded hillsides and ravines.

For a small wild creature, maquis thickets can be

impenetrable protection against disturbance. Within the maquis, the cats find ample prey. Like its domestic relatives, the wildcat is the scourge of small rodents and ground birds. Rabbits, songbirds, and even fish also perish under the creature's claw and teeth. Hunting mostly by dark, the wildcat creeps within a few yards of its victim, just as a tabby stalks a bird in the backyard. Then, with a rush, the creature pounces on its victim, seizing it in its claws. By day, wildcats usually rest in the brush or in the branches of a tree.

While human activities have hurt the wildcat in Europe, they have helped the creature in Africa. Agricultural development—particularly grain farming—has increased the numbers of rodents in many areas, improving hunting prospects for the cat. At night, cornfields draw large numbers of hungry wildcats.

Wildcats spend most of their time apart from one another, except when it is time to procreate. Their mating rituals resemble those of their domestic relatives. Mating takes place in the late winter in temperate climates, year-round elsewhere. After about two months, the young are born in a cave, badger burrow, hollow log, or tree cavity. As many as five kittens have been recorded in the wildcat litter. Generally, however, the creature has two or three young. The kittens grow quickly and hunt as well as adults before they are a year old.

Related to the wildcat are four feline species that are very similar but that have special adaptations for their surroundings, which differ from the woodlands favored by the wildcat. The jungle cat (*Felis chaus*), for instance, subsists largely on frogs—a perfectly natural diet since, despite its name, it lives in swamps, marshes, reedy fringes of lakes and streams, and waterside woodlands; one favorite habitat of this animal is the low, mature woodlands that grow along the Caspian Sea in northern Iran. It is not difficult to figure out why this feline is sometimes called "swamp cat."

The other three cats in the clan to which the tabby belongs occupy habitats vastly different from those of the jungle cat. The sand cat (*Felis margarita*), the black-footed cat (*Felis nigripes*), and the Chinese desert cat (*Felis bieti*)—as the names of two imply—live in regions that are parched and sandy. Secretive creatures native to remote places, these cats seldom cross paths with humans. Like some of the other small felines, the desert-dwelling relatives of the domestic cat are enigmas, largely unobserved by scientists.

Sand cats live deep in the Sahara and the Arabian

Peninsula as well as in the driest regions of the Middle East into Turkestan and Pakistan. The Chinese desert cat wanders the arid scrublands of northern China and Mongolia; the black-footed cat, the Kalahari and other deserts of southern Africa.

All three species have keen hearing, an adaptation common in predators that must hunt in the desert, where prey is scarce. The sound receptors in the inner ear are larger than usual for a cat, as are the ears proper. Moreover, thick mats of hair cover the soles of the feet to protect the cats against the searing sand and from bogging down in it.

Like most desert animals, these dry-country cats remain under cover during the heat of the day. A cavity under roots or in a rock pile suffices as a daytime refuge for the sand cat. For the black-footed cat, a hole in an abandoned termite mound provides a cool retreat. Once the chill blackness of the desert night descends, the cats creep silently from their cover, intently listening for the tiny scratches, skitterings, and shufflings that hint of the presence of a lizard, a mouse, or a beetle. So sensitive is the hearing of these cats that they can even detect prey underground. Once they have located prey, the felines stalk silently, then spring explosively.

It seems fitting that these small cats, native to remote deserts, hunt in the dark. They are, by and large, creatures of mystery, despite their familiar look as cousins of our house cats. There is, however, a subtly different aura to the wild members of the clan. As a wildcat stalks its prey, for example, it goes through the same motions as the domestic cat, but in every fluid move each tensing of muscle speaks of additional grace, extra power—and a fierceness that allows no mistake. A wildcat may be almost a mirror image of the tabby, but it remains a creature that has not surrendered its wildness.

101. *Its forest haunts destroyed, its numbers decimated by bounties and relentless persecution because of real and imagined threats to game and domestic animals, the wildcat has vanished from much of Europe. In the British Isles, for instance, it survives today only on the rocky, wind-blasted highlands of Scotland. Although they prey on grouse and kill an occasional deer fawn, wildcats are valued by landowners in this more enlightened age because they help control populations of rabbits and rodents. Felis silvestris is an agile climber and may spend its day sleeping in a hollow tree or soaking up the sun on a limb. The wildcat begins its hunt in the twilight hour, stalking a network of hunting paths that covers a home territory of about 125 acres.*

102 *and* **103.** *The African wildcat,
which some scientists consider a
separate species* (Felis libyca), *has
a diet that varies from a 9-pound
rodent known as the springhare to
snakes, spiders, and centipedes.
Unlike its European kin, which
has retreated to remote refuges
under pressure of civilization, the
African wildcat has thrived on the
burgeoning rodent populations that
have followed conversion of native
savanna to grainfields.*

104 and **105.** *Wildcats lead a lonely life except at mating time, when several males will gather around a female in heat. Such encounters tend to be noisy and often violent. Two or three young is the typical litter size, and the blind kittens weigh about an ounce and a half at birth. They will open their eyes at ten days, nurse for a month, make their first excursions from the den a day or two later, and begin to hunt with their mother when they are three months old.*

106 *overleaf. The schooling period for young wildcats is brief: By the age of five months they will be left to their fast-learned and inherited skills to survive. The hunting technique of a wildcat is mirrored by a domestic tabby stalking a songbird or a mouse. The feline creeps close to its prey, then strikes with lightning-fast leaps.*

108. *Speed is the hallmark of both the cheetah (Acinonyx jubatus)—the fastest animal on Earth—and its smaller cousin, the caracal (Felis caracal). But while the caracal can easily run down a small gazelle, it is best known for its bird-catching skills. Springing into a flock of feeding doves, its forepaws a blur, the caracal can knock down a dozen birds before the panicked survivors escape. It can leap 6 feet into the air to snatch feathered prey. An agile climber, it raids treetop nests and the roosts of colonial birds; not even the martial eagle is safe from this fearless hunter.*

The Leapers

The Aberdare Mountains soar from the central highlands
of Kenya to an altitude of almost 13,000 feet. Jungle-like
rain forest covers the lower slopes of these scenic peaks.
Colobus monkeys, with coats of lush black-and-white fur,
gambol in the trees, and bushbuck antelope hide in
thickets on the shadowed ground. With altitude, the rain
forest gives way to tree ferns, then to stands of bamboo
so thick a person can hardly walk through them. Bongo
antelope, with white harnesses of striping and lyre-
shaped horns, haunt the bamboo.

Above the bamboo, at the top of the mountains, a
different sort of realm is unveiled when the wind sweeps
back the fog. As far as the eye can see are vast, boggy
moorlands, with flowers growing among the tough
grasses. Reminiscent of the moors of Scotland, this
world atop the Aberdares also has a touch of wildness
that is peculiarly African. In the distance, a white
curtain of cascading water can be seen as it tumbles
hundreds of feet over a stark precipice. The moors are
studded with mossy outcroppings of rock and craggy
ridges, laced by cold streams harboring trout, and
covered here and there with giant heaths bearded with
hanging lichens. It is a remote world, vastly different
from the savannas that rim the Aberdare country.

Wild creatures haunt these moorlands. In the chill
dampness under gray skies, elephants forage amid the
giant heaths, and black rhinoceroses browse on the
tussocks of bog grass. When the wind pushes aside the
mist, massive eland antelope, big as oxen, materialize.
Bush duikers and black-fronted duikers—tiny antelope—
hide in the myriad thickets scattered across the moors.
Leopards sometimes emerge from the lower forests to

prowl this high country. Harriers and African marsh owls fly low over the landscape searching for prey. Sunbirds and chats flit about, adding flashes of color to the scenery. Secretary birds, on long legs, stride across the ground. In the grasses, partridge-like birds called montane francolins putter over the ground after seeds. One such flock is feeding among the tussocks near a boggy patch of ground. Hidden in the grass, not far from the birds, is a long-legged, medium-size cat, tawny yellow with dark spots that merge into stripes along its neck and back. It is a slim but powerful-looking animal, with legs that are now tensed beneath it in a crouch. Moving with great economy, the cat creeps closer and closer to the covey of francolins. It creeps a few inches at a time, freezes, then resumes its stalk. Close to the birds, the cat halts. Its muscles tense. Finally, it explodes into action. With a sudden burst of speed, the feline is in the midst of the birds. They flush explosively into the air, scattering in every direction. One of the birds shoots over the cat, five feet above its head. Like lightning, the cat hurls itself into the air and, with a swipe of its paws almost too fast for the eye to see, snatches the francolin.

The serval (*Felis serval*) is one of two cats famed for their ability to leap high into the air and snag birds on the wing. The other is the caracal (*Felis caracal*). Both are about the same size, between thirty and forty pounds, slim but strongly built, with unusually long legs, similar to those of the cheetah but relatively longer in the upper leg and shorter in the foreleg. This trait contributes to the marvelous leaping ability of servals and caracals. Shooting off the ground like a steel spring uncoiling, one of these cats can easily reach a bird perched on a limb ten feet from the ground. A caracal or a serval can even take several birds out of the air in a single bound.

Like the cheetah, the serval and the caracal live by speed. Neither is as fast as the cheetah, but both surpass it in terms of overall nimbleness. Their combination of speed and grace make them among the most deadly hunters of the medium-size cats. Like cheetahs, caracals were once trained by Indian and Arabic nobility as hunting animals, used to chase down small antelope, hares, and birds. The owners of the cats would sometimes wager on which of their beasts would be the more successful hunter. The winner was the cat that knocked down the most birds during one attack. Totals sometimes numbered a dozen per cat.

Caracals are flat-headed and brownish red in color, with

tassled black ears; the name "caracal" comes from the Turkish word *karakal*, which means "black ear." They are essentially creatures of wide-open countryside, but they also frequent the scattered acacia woodlands and thorn scrub of Africa. On that continent, caracals range across the savanna belt, which stretches from the west coast eastward above the vast central African rain forest, throughout the east African savanna country, and in the deserts of southern Africa. A few caracals also roam North Africa and such parts of the Middle East as the sand-dune country of central and southern Iran. In India, where caracals once sat at the feet of princes, only scant numbers of the sleek cats remain.

The serval, unlike the caracal, inhabits both open and forested country and is strictly an African animal. It lives throughout most of sub-Saharan Africa, except for the thickest jungle and the driest desert, and is commonly found in moorlands such as those atop the Aberdares. Servals, for example, live in the high moorlands of Mt. Kenya where they prowl amidst the giant lobelias, heaths, and senecio plants.

West Africa is the home of a small subspecies of the serval, the servaline, or small-spotted serval. Its gray-tinged coat is marked with tiny spots, which make it look speckled. The servaline inhabits West African savannas and forest edges.

Although servals and caracals are not as secretive as some of the other smaller cats, scientists have not observed them extensively in the wild. Much of what is known about their reproductive habits, for example, comes from observations of zoo animals.

Because they are warm-climate animals, servals and caracals do not seem to have definite mating seasons, at least in the equatorial portions of their ranges. Caracals in southern Africa, however, seem to bear young mostly in July and August, while those slightly to the north have their offspring during the seasons that correspond to fall and early winter in the North Temperate Zone. The den in which the female gives birth is often an old porcupine burrow or a crevice in rocks. Both species carry their young—usually numbering two or three—for about two and a half months. The kits remain with their mother for about a year before she abandons them.

Servals and caracals are thought by many scientists to be closely related, although some biologists consider the latter to be closer to the lynx. (The caracal of North Africa, in fact, is known as the Barbary lynx.) Whether or not the two cats are close relatives, they share certain behavioral traits. If a caracal or a serval is being chased by people with hounds, it will scramble into the branches; servals also escape by swimming. If these cats are cornered, they also can counterattack furiously and, fighting with fang and claw, can easily kill dogs. So much respect is given the serval for its fighting ability that traditionally its pelt has been worn by chiefs of several African tribes. Caracals have attacked and injured humans who have boxed them into a corner.

Although both caracals and servals feed on a variety of small creatures ranging from rodents, lizards, and ground birds to small antelope, caracals regularly kill even larger animals. Caracals can catch and kill African antelope of moderate size, such as reedbuck and blackbuck. They also kill blackbuck in India, although today both the cat and the antelope are rare there. In the Middle East, caracals often prey on wild goats and sheep, the same victims sought by leopards. They sometimes take ostriches, whose kick can disembowel even a big cat, while the birds are nesting, and can even kill eagles perched on the ground.

Both felines can run down gazelles over a short distance, in this respect approaching the ability of the cheetah. But it is in pursuit of smaller arboreal or flying creatures that the caracal and serval most dramatically display their adaptive hunting talents. Few predators, for instance, are so adept at catching hyraxes, rabbit-size creatures of Africa and the Middle East that can scramble about trees and pop in and out of rock piles with elfin nimbleness. Servals, although primarily ground animals, can leap into the branches to capture hyraxes, and caracals track the creatures in the crevices of rocky slopes.

To find their prey, servals and caracals seem to use both eyes and ears effectively. They sometimes crouch in the grass, ears cocked, listening for the movements of rodents and other small animals among the roots. Once the prey is detected, the cat leaps upon it with speed and certainty, in its agile movements providing yet another example of how felines the world over have adapted to a variety of life styles that have evolved since prehistory.

113. *Those startling ears gave the caracal its name, which in Turkish means "black-eared." They are long, tapered to a sharp point, covered with black fur on the outside, and tipped with tufts that betray the caracal's close relationship to the lynx of northern forests. Haunting dry woodland, savanna, and scrub, the caracal is found throughout Africa, from the Mediterranean Sea to the Cape of Good Hope; across the Middle East; and into India, where for centuries the cat has been tamed and trained to hunt for humans. But in many areas it has become rare because of the fur trade's demand for the caracal's luxurious pelt.*

114 *overleaf. Caracal kittens curl up against their mother. The litter may be as many as six, most typically three, and their den will likely be an old porcupine burrow or a secluded rock crevice. The vocalizations of the caracal suggest a domestic cat: assorted meows, growls, hisses. One wildlife expert's pet caracal purred contentedly if given a saucer of milk.*

116 *and* **117;** **118** *overleaf. Batlike ears, long legs, a profusion of dark spots, and a ringed tail—assemble those characteristics and you have the African cat known as the serval (Felis serval). Solitary and nocturnal, this handsome feline stalks the grassy edges of savanna streams and marshes across most of the continent. It is also found on the foggy mountain moorlands of Kenya, where black servals are occasionally seen.*

122 *overleaf. Like the caracal, the serval is adept at leaping into the air to catch birds on the wing. But a serval that appears to be jumping about aimlessly in the grass is really trying to trick a hare into leaving its hiding place. The serval stands 2 feet high at the shoulders and weighs perhaps 30 pounds. The female will raise two litters a year.*

120 *and* **121.** *One writer termed the serval's ears "preposterous," but its hearing is so acute that it can detect the slightest movement of a mouse or rat in the marsh grass. Small rodents and birds are the serval's usual prey, but the cat also hunts such game birds as guinea fowl and francolins and has been known to kill the smallest antelope. It will also climb high into the branches to raid the lairs of tree hyraxes.*

124. *On the grasslands of Kenya's Masai Mara reserve, a cheetah (Acinonyx jubatus) uses a termite mound as a lookout post to spot potential prey. If a mound or rock isn't handy, the cat may climb a tree to gain a vantage point. Approaching a herd of antelope, a cheetah probably will make no attempt to conceal itself. The first animal to bolt will be pursued, the rest of the herd ignored. But the cheetah's rush can be thwarted if the intended victim dashes back into the herd.*

Survival of the Fleetest

Heavy-lidded, a cheetah (*Acinonyx jubatus*) dozes atop the hard-baked soil of a termite mound, bathed in the still-cool sunlight of an East African morning. Periodically, the cat's tail twitches, an ear flicks away a fly, shoulder muscles shift almost imperceptively. The sleepy cheetah nevertheless remains alert, ready to bolt at undue disturbance despite its languid repose.

A resting cheetah gives the impression of studied indolence and supreme ease. But the lean lines of its wiry body proclaim that when stirred into action the long-legged, spotted cat moves like lightning. For a few hundred yards, the cheetah can travel faster than anything else on four legs, reaching speeds in the vicinity of seventy miles an hour.

The cheetah on the termite mound, however, is heavy with unborn cubs, her body's sleek contours blurred. Within weeks, she will give birth to cubs sired about two months before.

The female had announced her readiness to mate by repeatedly marking trees, shrubs, grass, and other vegetation with urine as she traveled through a portion of her home range—a territory that covers more than 400 square miles of grassland, thorn scrub, and scattered batches of trees. Squatting, she had sprayed her scent backward, drenching the vegetation and leaving an unmistakable message to nearby males.

The advertisement had quickly drawn a male. Striding over the grasslands, he had followed the trail of the female. At each scent mark, he had lowered his muzzle and sniffed with growing eagerness. Trying to attract the female, he had uttered plaintive yelps that echoed in the clear air.

125

A quarter mile away, resting in the tall grass, the female had heard the calls of the male. Rising to her feet, she had scanned the flat landscape. A few moments later, the male had appeared, at first covering ground with an easy gait but then bursting into a gallop. Mating had taken but seconds, and then the cats had lolled luxuriously in the grass.

For more than a day, the two cats had remained together, repeating their mating act but for the most part lying near each other. The female had appeared to be relaxed, while the male had intently eyed her, seemingly attentive to her moods. With mating assured after so many couplings, the female had had enough of her consort and was ready to slip away from him. Indeed, after some hours more, she had casually wandered away, vanishing into the vast savannas.

The male had also moved off, surveying the landscape for prey. Later, he may have remained alone, for most cheetahs are solitary animals. However, small groups of males do form, and thus he may have joined a bachelor band, staying with them until it was time to mate again or until prey dwindled to the point that the group could not find enough food and dispersed.

When it is time to give birth, the female seeks the shelter of a dense thicket. She is constantly alert, for, heavy with young, she is an easy target for lions and leopards that might be tempted to take a smaller cat. Later, her cubs will be vulnerable to even more predators, not only other felines but also hyenas, which, contrary to popular belief, kill their own prey much more than they scavenge the leavings of others.

When the cubs—between two and six in a litter—are born, they remain hidden in the brush. They have a somewhat different coat from their mother, whose pelt is tawny yellow and dotted with round, black spots. The lower half of a cub's body is very dark, while the hair along its back and behind its neck is very light and long, resembling a mane. Possibly a throwback to some forgotten ancestor, the mane disappears in about three months, when the young are weaned.

For several weeks after they are born, the cubs remain under cover. Gradually, they begin to toddle after their mother. By two months of age, they have left their nursery and are traveling across the plains with their parent. At first, the mother leaves the young hidden while she hunts. On her return, she calls them with a soft signal that sounds like the chirp of a bird. When the cubs are ready to eat, the female regularly brings back prey for them. Sometimes she strips the victim of hide, making it easier for the cubs to get to the flesh.

When young, the cubs are in danger from predators, because their mother is no match for a lion, a leopard, or a pack of hyenas. However, the cubs can utilize a refuge unavailable to adult cheetahs—trees. Unlike adults, cheetah cubs can climb because they have retractile claws, a trait that vanishes as they mature.

Before long, the cubs are sufficiently mobile to follow their mother as she hunts and to begin hunting themselves. Cheetahs prey on a variety of plains game and smaller animals. Among their targets are smaller antelope such as reedbuck, impala, and Thomson's and Grant's gazelles. Cheetahs kill adult gazelles but prefer fawns because they are far easier to catch. The young of most antelope are prey for the cheetah, as are smaller creatures such as hares.

The cheetah begins its hunt by stalking, its body hugging the ground until it is as close as possible to its victim. When the cat is between six and fifty feet of its prey, it erupts from cover and runs directly at its target. Watching a cheetah streak after a victim, it is hard to believe the cat is made of living flesh; its body works more like a flexible coil of steel. So supple is the cheetah that as it runs its frame undergoes tremendous contortions, yet the grace of its movements is not disrupted. As the cat's long legs are drawn under the body, the back arches upward. Then the legs reach out in a monumental stretch, and the back snaps toward the ground like a rubber band pulled to its furthest extent and released. The process hurls the cheetah forward at blinding speed.

One adaptation to the cheetah's method of catching prey is the animal's blunted claws, which resemble those of a dog. Because of its blunt claws the cheetah cannot turn with the agility of other cats, yet the traction they provide allows it to stay on the tail of a twisting, turning victim like a heat-seeking missile after a fleeing aircraft. The cat's long tail helps it to balance, making up for the lack of sharp claws. The cheetah can run faster than a gazelle, which has a top speed somewhat over forty miles an hour, but not for long. If the prey can manage to stay out of the cat's reach for about 500 yards, the cheetah—whose exertions have expended its reserves of energy—gives up, panting.

Most of the time the cheetah closes in on the fleeing prey, lashes out with a front paw, and swats its intended meal off balance. Some scientists believe that the cheetah's dewclaw hooks into the victim and helps take it off its feet. As the prey falls, the cheetah is on it in a flash, clamping its jaws down on the throat and holding tight until the victim strangles. One of the reasons that cheetahs shy away from large prey is that their jaws are not as powerful as those of other cats their size.

When training her young to hunt, a mother cheetah sometimes will capture an animal—usually a fawn—without killing it. Then she will release it in front of her cubs so that they may practice. It seems cruel, perhaps, but only in human terms. If the young cheetahs do not learn to hunt, they will perish. And in the long run, the absence of cheetahs subtracts from the balance of nature in the plains community to the detriment of all, including the species hunted by this swift cat.

Cheetahs require large amounts of range. Scientists estimate, for example, that about 1,000 of the cats roam the 9,600 square miles of the vast Serengeti ecosystem, including Tanzania's famed Serengeti National Park and its environs. Parks such as the Serengeti are essential to the survival of this cat.

The story of the decline of the cheetah is similar to that of many other cats. Habitat destruction and excessive hunting for the cheetah's pelt caused it to vanish from much of its original range, which covered most of Africa and the Middle East through Iran, Soviet Turkestan, and Afghanistan to central and southern India. Cheetahs have not been seen in India since 1951, and they may be gone from the Soviet Union and Arabia. They had been surviving in parts of rugged and remote northwestern Iran, but since the Iranian revolution their condition is unknown. Thought to be extinct in Israel, the cheetah may emerge from the shadows there in the same way the Sinai leopard has. In that country, scientists have recently found traces of animals they believe may be cheetahs. Whether or not cheetahs do live there—or if they do in sufficient numbers to survive—only time will tell.

The territory occupied by cheetahs in Africa has dwindled, though not as much as the cat's Asian range. Once abundant in South Africa, cheetahs are now reduced to scattered pockets there, chiefly in game sanctuaries. Populations are near the danger mark in Ethiopia and Somalia. Only in Kenya, Tanzania, and adjacent parts of East Africa do cheetahs remain in significant numbers—and still they are only a fragment of those that existed in the past. Without sound conservation measures, the fastest being on four legs will not be able to outrace extinction.

129. *With its habitat being turned into cropland to feed Africa's burgeoning population and its prey species declining, the cheetah is considered by conservationists to be among the most endangered cats on earth. Cheetahs produce more young than any other big cat, but seven out of ten cubs will perish from malnutrition, disease, and predation. The cheetah once was found from Africa across the Middle East to India, where the last of its kind was killed in 1951. Only token populations survive today in the Soviet Union, Iran, and Arabia.*

130 and **131.** *For the first few weeks of their lives, cheetah cubs hide while their mother hunts, feeding on regurgitated meat when she returns. Very young cheetahs seem to be protected from predators by an unusual color pattern—silver-gray on the top of the head and back, dark fur below—that mimics the honey badger, a small and utterly fearless carnivore. Honey badgers can easily scatter a pack of hyenas and have been known to leave a Cape buffalo with fatal wounds. The cubs—an average of four to a litter, although five or six is not an uncommon number—are weaned by the age of three months and assume the cheetah's normal spotted coat.*

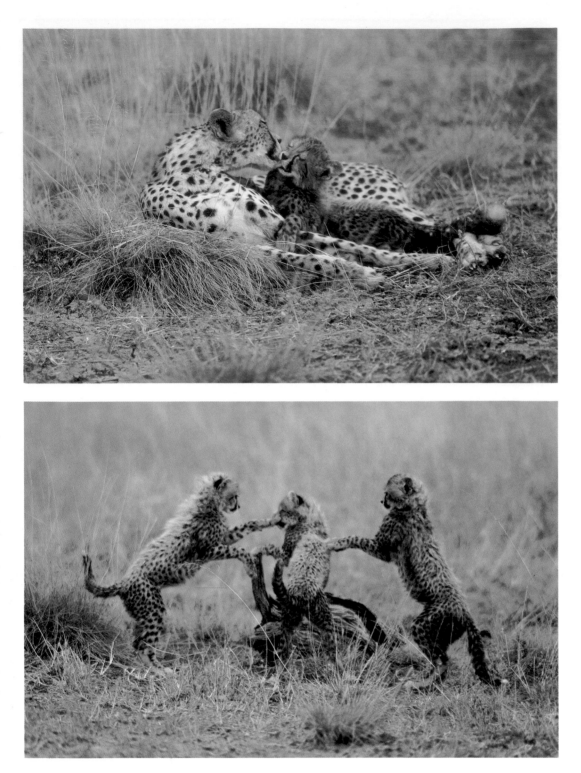

132 and **133.** *A female cheetah purrs loudly while grooming her cubs, and she will summon them to the site of a kill with birdlike chirps. Unlike a leopard or lion, however, the cheetah cannot roar. Cheetah cubs learn their hunting technique through play, practice, and observation. Their mother may bring back a live antelope and let them chase it, but unless the cubs have watched adult cheetahs in action, they will not know how to make the kill.*

134 *overleaf. By the time they are a year old, young cheetahs are competent hunters, although they will stay by their parent's side a few months longer. In the wild, their life span will be four or five years.*

136. *In their shaded hideout, cheetah cubs feast on a Thomson's gazelle brought "home" by their mother. Cheetahs by custom drag their prey to cover, eat their fill, and leave the carcass, for they are unable to stand their ground against hyenas or lions. They forfeit perhaps one-fourth of their kills to scavengers and sometimes lose their lives to the bigger cats.*

137. *Under the expert eye of its parent, a half-grown cheetah cub has killed a Thomson's gazelle. Later it wrestles playfully with another cub. Unlike other large cats, the cheetah has short and small canine teeth and is unable to quickly disptach its prey in typical feline fashion by biting into the spine.*

138 and **139**. *The fastest animal on earth, the cheetah is a sprinter, not an endurance runner. It begins its pursuit of prey at a distance of from 100 to 200 yards, and from a standing start, the cheetah can reach a speed of forty-five miles per hour in two seconds flat. Its top speed is seventy mph, faster by far than a champion racehorse. But after a quarter mile the cheetah is through, winded and panting. If it has not made a kill, the cat is out of the game for a half hour or more.*

140 *overleaf. A yearling zebra is about the largest prey that a cheetah can manage. Unlike the leopard, the cheetah's body is designed for fast pursuit, not brute power: Its legs are long and slender, the heart and lungs oversize. Small antelope, namely Thomson's gazelles and impalas, are the cheetah's usual victims. The fleeing animal is tumbled off balance when the cat hooks one dewclaw, or "thumb," into its flank, then strangled by a crushing bite to its throat—a process that may take half an hour.*

142 *overleaf. In an uncharacteristic display of bravura, a cheetah tries to rout vultures that have settled about its kill. The smaller cat's timidity when challenged by a hungry lion is quite understandable, but even a determined gang of these feathered scavengers can drive a cheetah from its meal. Since cheetahs do not cache or defend a kill, they must take fresh prey every day.*

144 and **145; 146** *overleaf. Unlike the solitary leopard, the cheetah apparently welcomes the presence of others of its kind. At times groups of males hunt together with a leader who chooses the prey, and several groups will follow the seasonal herd migrations. Individual male cheetahs do not claim exclusive hunting territories, although they leave one-time scent marks that tell others that a particular area is taken for the day.*

148. *Most commonly seen in India, Java, and Malaysia, the melanistic form of the leopard (Panthera pardus) once was thought to be a separate species. "Black panthers," we now know, prowl the dark rain forests where they are almost invisible, the rosette pattern of their coats obscured except in bright light. Similarly, the tawny, spotted leopard of Africa is well camouflaged in its sun-washed thornbush haunts. Melanistic leopards are rare on the African continent except in the Ethiopian highlands.*

Bold Hunters

Streams of crystal water cascade over the rocky cliffs of the En-gedi oasis overlooking the western shore of the Dead Sea in Israel. A natural garden, En-gedi boasts lush tropical vegetation, such as salvadora and morgina, found nowhere else in the country. In biblical times, David sought refuge from Saul here among the "craggy rocks. . . . accessible only to wild goats." The wild goats, or ibex, still scramble over the crags of En-gedi, now a nature reserve. These nimble creatures are seen by the hundreds of thousands of visitors who tour the historic oasis each year. Occasionally, visitors glimpse another wild creature that, like the goats, is mentioned in the Bible but until a few years ago was believed to be extinct. Lazing on the rocks, perhaps prowling the edge of a precipice, a great spotted cat can be seen, unconcerned by the proximity of so many humans. This cat of En-gedi is the Sinai leopard (*Panthera pardus jarvisi*), a species of the fierce spotted feline that roves the Old World from Africa to the eastern rim of Asia. Until the 1970s, scientists believed the leopard of Israel was another creature that had passed into extinction. Gradually, however, it became apparent that at least a few leopards had survived. The evidence came in the form of, first, tracks and scat, then ibex kills, and finally sightings of the cat. By the 1980s, Israeli scientists were certain that leopards roved the entire country, including the barren wastes of the Negev Desert. The numbers of the cats, moreover, seemed to be increasing. The reappearance of the leopard in Israel is a result of the government's ambitious habitat and wildlife conservation program. Throughout the country, wildlife reserves were set aside, and the scant numbers of surviving wild creatures, such as the ibex, were protected and managed. As the ibex returned, so did the leopards, which find the goats a ready source of food. The astonishing resilience with which the leopard has emerged from the shadows testifies not only to the sound conservation efforts of the Israeli government but even more to the spotted cat's most important quality: It is above all a survivor. At least as adaptable as the cougar geographically and environmentally, the leopard even adjusts remarkably well to the presence of humans. On the outskirts of Nairobi, Kenya, for example, leopards regularly raid suburban backyards for dogs, a favorite prey, and sometimes even loll unabashedly on the roofs of carports.

Although leopards sometimes allow themselves to be seen, they are for the most part elusive. One large male leopard observed by scientists lived in a large gorge on the flank of Ethiopia's Simian Escarpment in an area flooded with humans, many of them armed with rifles. The leopard's refuge was only a hundred or so yards from farmland. Yet nightly it emerged, preyed on livestock, and returned to its haven undetected— demonstrating that leopards living near large human populations become even more secretive than they normally are in the wild. Moreover, they seldom use their voices and, as far as possible, seek refuge in rocky ravines or in uplands where people have little reason to venture. The leopard's usual custom of hunting by night also helps it avoid people.

In Sri Lanka, however, the spotted cats may hunt during the day because there the leopard is the most formidable mammalian predator. Leopards also seem to hunt primarily by day in the Judean Desert of Israel, possibly because its most important prey, ibex and hyraxes, are diurnal. When clouds mask the glare of the desert sun, leopards often are abroad all day; when skies are clear, however, the midday heat usually drives them under cover.

Cover seems to be a prerequisite if leopards are to survive in their varied habitats. These felines range all the way from the Caucasus of Turkey to China and Siberia, southern Asia and Arabia, and across almost all of Africa. Their habitats include snowy mountain peaks, baking deserts, thorn scrub, jungles, and temperate hardwood forests. Whatever their habitat, however, leopards shun open areas where they are exposed to the eyes of their prey. On savannas, for instance, they hug tree-lined watercourses, and in the desert they are likely to inhabit twisted canyons and rocky hillsides.

The leopard's coat—yellowish with black spots—provides natural camouflage that helps it stay out of sight. The markings of the leopard blend well with vegetation and rough, rocky backgrounds. Leopards living in forested areas are often smaller than those of open country. This is not surprising, for a smaller creature can maneuver more easily than a larger one in a heavily wooded area. Woodlands leopards are also more darkly spotted, which helps conceal them in the shadows of the forest. In contrast, leopards of sunlit plains and deserts have lighter spots. Both males and females have the same color pattern and closely resemble each other, although in general females are smaller.

Concealment also helps leopards to capture prey. Usually they hunt alone except in and around breeding season, which is year-round in the tropics and in late winter in northern areas. When male and female leopards link up, the pair often hunts together. The male remains with the family for several months, helping provide for the young with the fruits of his hunting. Leopards are agile and fast but lack the endurance to run down fleet or nimble prey. Thus, they often lie in wait along trails on which creatures such as wild boar, antelope, or deer travel. When the prey comes within a distance of three or four yards, the cat springs and seizes it in its steel-like claws. Large victims are killed with a bite to the neck, or the leopard may strangle the creature by closing its jaws on the windpipe or severing the spine with a crushing bite through the nape.

The leopard seems to be one of the more fastidious of the big cats. After it makes a kill, it removes the victim's stomach and intestinal organs, which may then be buried under vegetation or earth. Only then does it begin to feed on the carcass. If the prey is a larger meal than the leopard can handle at one sitting, the cat will return to it later and continue to feed until all is consumed.

Pound for pound leopards are the strongest felines, yet they seldom weigh more than 150 pounds. Remarkably, these short-legged, heavy-bodied cats can bring down antelope several times their weight. Leopards even haul the carcasses of victims much larger than they are into trees, where they cache them safely.

Because it is easier for the cat to kill domestic livestock, and because it may kill more than it needs, the leopard is unfortunately at cross purposes with humans. Even so, the adaptability of the leopard and its ability to persist even in a fast-developing nation such as Israel bode well for its future.

Another cat, which also bears the name leopard, has

none of the adaptability of its Sinai cousin. This is the snow leopard (*Uncia uncia*), rarest by far of the large cats and by anyone's measure the most beautiful. The snow leopard is adapted to a very specific environment, the bleak highlands of central Asia, a realm of bone-chilling temperatures, fierce winds, soaring cliffs, and jagged mountain peaks.

Long, lush fur as well as a thick tail insulate the cat against the cold. Like the lynx, the snow leopard has large, hairy feet for support on snow and traction on ice. This eighty-pound cat can leap prodigiously—up to fifteen yards—not only horizontally but vertically, a trait that enables it to reach high ledges without climbing. Ironically, it is the snow leopard's superb adaptation to only one place that threatens its existence, for it can adapt to no other. And even this remote sanctuary is endangered. Humans with livestock are sweeping up the lower slopes of the mountains where the snow leopards descend when winter envelops the grim heights. In addition, vegetation is decreasing and, with it, the wild sheep and other wild ungulates on which the snow leopard feeds. When the cat turns to livestock, it is hunted and killed, as it has been constantly for its gorgeous pelt, which is stone gray with dark markings. From observations of snow leopards in captivity, scientists know the gestation period is between ninety-six and one hundred days. The cubs—between one and four per litter—are born in a cave or a crevice in the rocks, usually in the pine-forested lower slopes. There the young are sheltered from the elements, and prey is more abundant than on the higher peaks.

Young snow leopards begin hunting alongside their mother by summer's end. As winter approaches, they follow the mountain sheep and other creatures on which they feed down into the sheltered valleys. The young stay with their mother for a year and a half, even though they reach full size before that time. Then they leave to patrol the highlands alone.

Conservationists have mounted a worldwide campaign to save the snow leopard, but the future of this cat is very much in doubt. Scientists estimate that only about 250 snow leopards survive in Pakistan, perhaps 300 more in Nepal, and another 300 in Mongolia. About another 200 are in zoos, where biologists are trying to breed them for possible reintroduction in the wild. Even if this plan is successful, however, the snow leopard will have a hard time surviving if it and its habitat are not protected.

153. *Without challenge, the most beautiful big cat in the world is the snow leopard* (Uncia uncia). *Regrettably, it is also our rarest large feline, a dubious distinction due in part to the species' narrow ecological niche—the cold, rocky fastnesses of the Himalayas and lesser mountain ranges that reach northward to Siberia and Mongolia. But it is an extraordinary coat that has caused the snow leopard's numbers to be reduced to the mere hundreds. Pale gray, marked with spots and rosettes, the luxuriant fur is thick and long to provide insulation in the frigid alpine environment. Thus countless snow leopards were killed to meet the demands of the fashion industry, and illegal traffic persists today despite an international embargo and national laws protecting the cat. The snow leopard's lofty, frigid haunts have led to other unique traits as well. Its tail, thickly furred and as long as its body, is used to maintain balance on steep climbs and as a warm muffler when the cat curls up to sleep. And its paws are oversize for walking atop deep snow.*

154 *overleaf. By tradition, the leopard is a secretive, nocturnal hunter. But it is not unusual to see* Panthera pardus *stalking prey in daylight on Africa's wildlife preserves. There, under protection, the leopard has become increasingly diurnal in its habits. Leopards, by necessity, also hunt under the harsh sun of the Negev Desert of Israel, for their prey are ibex and rock-dwelling hyraxes that are active by day.*

156 *above and left. Pulling down a 200-pound African bush pig* (Potamochoerus porcus) *twice its size, a leopard finishes its victim with a spine-crushing bite through the nape of the neck. A complete list of the leopard's prey species would be a long one, including birds, rodents, hares, fish, primates, and even pythons. Prey larger than bush pigs and medium-size antelope is left to the lion and tiger. Leopards are especially fond of dogs, not only wild jackals but also domestic canines brazenly snatched from natives' huts.*

158 *and* **159.** *Like playful kittens, two leopards frolic in a shallow river in India's Dudhwa National Park. A pair of leopards will hunt together during the mating season, but they split up before the cubs are born, the female to raise her offspring—a two-year undertaking —the male to proclaim his territory with roars, clawed tree trunks, and scent stations.*

160 and **161.** *Whether swimming a jungle river or reclining on a lofty limb, the leopard is a picture of power and grace. And no big feline is more adaptable in its choice of habitat—the leopard is equally at home in rain-drenched forests, rocky alpine heights, or arid lands where the cat's only sources of moisture are water-filled fruit, called desert melons, or the blood of its victims.*

162 *overleaf. In areas with abundant prey and no other large predators, such as the African rain forests, the leopard population may be as dense as one cat per square mile. But the competition between leopards and lions is intense, and on the plains of the Serengeti there may be only one leopard for every eight or ten square miles of habitat. Indeed, scientists have found that leopards seek out river-bottom forests as a refuge from lions, for the larger cats will try to claim their kills. In Asia, the tiger—four times its size—is the leopard's competitor for prey, and never are both cats common in one area.*

164 and 165; 166 overleaf. In places
where food might be stolen by lions,
hyenas, or wild dogs, a leopard
will grab its kill by the neck and
haul it into a tree, out of the reach
of scavengers. Animals as large as
a Thomson's gazelle or reedbuck
will be cached in the branches and
fed upon for days. Leopards in
Asia, plagued by tigers, follow the
same practice. But in the rain
forests of Africa, where the spotted
cats live free of harassment, kills
are rarely stored aboveground.

168. *"El Tigre" was the name that early Spanish explorers gave to the jaguar* (Panthera onca), *and over the centuries the largest cat in the New World has been called "the tiger" by Latin Americans. Indians, on the other hand, knew it as "jaguara," a word that described its technique of bringing down prey with a single deadly leap from ambush, and that name also stuck. There is evidence that jaguars still prowled the southeastern part of the United States when the first European settlers arrived; from fossils, we know they were present in late prehistoric times. But today the jaguar is rarely seen north of the Mexican border.*

Czar of the Amazon

Day is breaking in the Amazon rain forest. Howler monkeys greet the dawn with thunderous roars. In the towering forest canopy, parrots and macaws screech, and toucans begin hunting for fruit amid the leaves. Shadowed by the canopy overhead and hidden in a clump of low brush, a great spotted cat crouches quietly beside a deer trail. The patchwork of dark rosettes that cover its buffy coat blend subtly with the dappled sunlight filtering through the leafy roof far above.

As its keen hearing picks up a faint sound ahead on trail, the cat tenses. Its steely shoulder muscles bunch, its body flattens closer to the ground. Warily moving down the trail, sniffing for a hint of danger, a brocket deer approaches the cat. Nearer and nearer comes the deer, unaware that it is walking into an ambush laid by the supreme mammalian predator of the American tropics, the jaguar (*Panthera onca*).

The deer, upwind from the jaguar, fails to scent the cat. After a few minutes, the brocket ambles in range of the fierce hunter. In a sudden explosion of raw fury, the sleek jaguar hurtles through the air, knocking down the brocket. With lightning speed the cat fastens its huge fangs onto the skull of the deer, piercing the bone and entering the brocket's brain—killing it instantly.

Grim and savage as such a scene may be, it dramatizes the immense power and ferocity of the largest cat of the Americas, third in size among felines behind the lion and the tiger. The jaguar can be every bit as awesome as its two Old World cousins. Heavily muscled, weighing up to 350 pounds, although usually smaller, the jaguar takes its victim with more primal violence than any of the other wild cats.

Lions and tigers, for instance, usually stalk their prey on the ground and then rush it. Jaguars, so far as is known, wait in ambush and then fall upon their victims with a mighty leap. The name *jaguar*, in fact, comes from an American Indian word, *jaguara*, which means "a beast that kills its prey with one bound."

The jaguar is a superb killing machine. Other big cats kill animals of moderate to large size by fastening their fangs into the throat of the victim and strangling it. The jaguar's approach is more basic and direct: It crushes the skull of its prey, which includes animals as large as cattle. There is more to the jaguar's bite, however, than pure brute force. With unerring accuracy, the cat's teeth hone in on both sides of the skull, where the bone is relatively thin.

Throughout much of this fierce cat's range, on the grassy pampas of southern South America, where jungles have been cleared to provide grazing land, the cat preys most often on cattle. As a result, the jaguar has a reputation as a killer of livestock. Many ranchers and farmers disregard laws designed to protect the jaguar, and they kill the cat on sight.

Laws also have been passed to protect the jaguar from hide hunters. From the 1950s to the 1970s, thousands of jaguar hides were shipped to markets in the United States and Europe from Central and South America. Today, the flow of pelts has been reduced dramatically, but some pelt-hunting continues. Although no one knows the exact population of jaguars, it is certain that the species cannot tolerate any such loss.

Since the nineteenth century, humans and their activities have pushed the jaguar out of the northern fringes of its range and confined it to Latin America. During historic times, jaguars roamed from the southwestern United States into Argentina, and earlier they extended northward to the central United States and east to Florida. Within the past century, however, they have been driven south of the United States border. Rarely, a cat may stray north into extreme southern Arizona.

Jaguars are not nearly as cosmopolitan in their choice of habitats as the other large American cat, the cougar. While they do exist in scrub, arid brush, and pampas, jaguars seldom roam far from water. On the pampas, for example, they tend to hover around swampy borders of river systems.

For the most part, jaguars are creatures of the forest, chiefly jungle. Roving some of the deepest jungles on earth, such as the Amazon rain forest, they have been observed less than any other big cat. Biologists have spent months trying to find them yet often have had to be content with studying their tracks and listening to their coughing roars, a series of powerful grunts. Recent studies, however, indicate that jaguars have a territorial system similar to that of tigers. One male holds a large territory, which includes the hunting grounds of several females. The territories of the females, moreover, often impinge on one another. A typical female holding is about fifteen square miles, although the size may vary considerably according to terrain and availability of prey.

Female jaguars, which are slightly smaller than males, bear young every two years. Some scientists believe that the male jaguar teams up with the female to rear the young, although this is by no means certain. Jaguar cubs —between two and four in a litter, but usually the former—are born after a gestation period of between 93 and 110 days. They arrive in the world covered with fuzzy brown fur that will yellow as they mature. Their young coats are dotted with dark spots that will be transformed into rosettes before the cubs are ready for life on their own.

Weighing two pounds and measuring slightly less than a foot and a half long, the jaguar cubs are blind at birth, but within a week or two they open their eyes. At first they see only the inside of the den, which may be a cave or a hollow under a fallen tree. Within a couple of months, however, the young jaguars will start hunting with their mother. They will remain with her for two years, at which time their weight will reach about 200 pounds. But they still will not be full size. It takes one or two more years before the young grow to the mature adult size.

Like the lion on the savannas of Africa, the jaguar stands at the top of the jungle food chain. The animals that regularly furnish its food testify to the cat's power and ferocity. Jaguars easily kill the capybara, the world's largest rodent, which can weigh as much as one hundred pounds. Deer are a dietary mainstay, as are tapirs, which can surpass the jaguar in size. A hungry jaguar will even plunge into water and attack a caiman, a feisty crocodilian that is itself a vicious predator. The cats also seize peccaries, piglike creatures with razor-sharp tusks and equally sharp tempers. Peccaries are found throughout most of the jaguar's range, and in some places they are a major food item for the cats. Hunting peccaries, however, can be risky. Often a jaguar must seek the safety of the trees when a herd of peccaries charges at it.

Jaguars also may hunt smaller creatures, such as turtles, frogs, mice, monkeys, and sloths. Generally, the prey of the jaguar are ground-dwelling animals. Because of its size, the jaguar is not as adept a climber as, say, the cougar or the leopard, but it can climb to the branches and sometimes lies in wait on a low-hanging limb for potential victims to pass beneath. When one does, the cat drops from above, instantly bringing the prey to the ground.

Once a victim is dead, the jaguar usually carries it off, thus demonstrating its tremendous strength. One cat is known to have hauled a full-grown horse for more than 200 feet and then carried it across a river.

The strength and ferocity of this animal symbolized frightening power to many of America's pre-Columbian peoples. Some 2,500 years ago, a stocky race of Mexican farmers, the Olmecs, carved myriad likenesses of jaguars in jade and stone as well as human figures with jaguar heads. Today, scholars think that the Olmecs may have been ruled by the members of a cult that took as its standard the ruler of the jungle, the jaguar.

The later Mayans, who were perhaps heirs of the Olmecs, dressed their high priests in the skins of jaguars, carved statues showing cats ready to pounce, and built jaguar temples in their sacred cities. Pre-Incan civilizations in South America worshiped feline gods and depicted them with carved and painted heads that seem to represent jaguars. Among the Aztecs of Mexico, those who waged war to capture humans for sacrifice, the Jaguar Knights, were considered heroes among warriors.

The jaguar no longer represents the awesome powers of the divine and the supernatural. But in the jungle, as long as it survives the pressures people have placed on it, the jaguar will still rule.

173. *The jaguar is an awesome hunting machine, and no animal—not even the caiman of Amazonian rivers—escapes its attention. The jaguar's most important prey are water-loving capybaras, the largest rodents in the world; tapirs, 500-pound swinelike beasts with huge snouts; and peccaries. The list also includes monkeys, deer, otters, and man's cattle and horses.*

174 *overleaf. A jaguar charges after its prey. Instead of biting or clawing a victim's neck in the manner of other big cats, a jaguar kills quickly by sinking its canines through the thinnest part of the skull into the brain. Indeed, a scientist studying fresh capybara kills found that a jaguar would insert one canine neatly into each ear of the 100-pound rodent.*

176 *and* **177.** *Jaguar courtship is a rough-and-tumble affair, as shown by this rare sequence of photographs. A male jaguar patrols a territory that includes the smaller hunting grounds of several females. The mating results in a litter of up to four kittens after a gestation period of three months. The cubs will keep to their natal den for six months before they venture out on hunts with their mother, and they will remain at her side for two years. But another two years will elapse before the young jaguars reach their full adult size—250 pounds for a male, 7 feet long from nose to tail; 200 pounds for a female.*

178 *overleaf. Jaguars are most likely to be found lurking near lowland rivers or lakes where prey is abundant. They will plunge into water without hesitation to grab a turtle or grapple with a ferocious caiman, New World cousin of the feared crocodile. But jaguar tracks have been discovered as high as 8,000 feet in the mountains of South America.*

180 and **181.** *The jaguar is the only cat in the Americas that can roar, a sound described by one scientist as "a series of hoarse barking coughs, an interval of about one second separating each expiratory effort." Thus El Tigre proclaims its territory to others of its kind.*

182 *overleaf. Although a bit larger, the jaguar is a mirror image of the Old World leopard, its yellow-to-tawny coat copiously marked with spots and rosettes. One small difference is that the jaguar usually has fewer and larger rosettes with dark spots in the center. As with the leopard, the demand among the rich and fashionable for fur coats made from the hides of beautifully marked wild cats led to countless thousands of jaguars being killed to supply markets in Europe and the United States. The jaguar is now protected, and international traffic in spotted cat pelts is banned. Black jaguars are not unusual, particularly in river-bottom rain forests.*

184. *In Mexico they call it the "otter cat," for the jaguarundi (Felis yagouaroundi) is distinctly weasel-like in appearance. Its head is small and flattened, its long and slender body slung low to the ground for prowling under dense brush in search of rodents and birds. Unlike other wildcats, it rarely climbs trees and usually hunts in the morning and early evening hours. The jaguarundi ranges from the southern United States border to Paraguay, and its habitat is lowland forests and thickets. Weighing 15 to 20 pounds, this tropical feline has fur that varies from foxy red to gunmetal blue.*

Tropical Acrobats

The Andean cat (*Felis jacobita*) is one of nine species of small cats found in the middle latitudes of the Americas. These cats inhabit desert, plains, and forest, as well as mountains. Among them is a dainty feline that is a tree acrobat and another that swims like an otter—as well as resembles one. All of these cats, at least as far as is known, are solitary except during the reproductive season. Most of them have seldom, if ever, been closely observed in the wild.

The land of the Andean cat looks like the broken rim of the world, where the high Andes rip jaggedly into the sky above Peru, Bolivia, Chile, and Argentina. Many of the peaks are snowcapped; others, at lower altitude, are barren, knife-edged, and craggy. For vast distances between the mountain ranges, an alpine plateau, the altiplano, stretches from one bleak horizon to another. Rippled by rocky ridges, the landscape is barren, save for bunches of brown, tough ichu grass. Windswept, alternately baked by sun and gripped by subfreezing cold, the land is unforgiving, an environment that places extreme stress on both human and beast.

Both, however, do live in this realm above the clouds. Most of the human population is American Indian in origin, descendants of the Incas and other peoples who built high civilizations in the mountains during past ages. Among the wildlife of the region—the great Andean condor, the graceful vicuna, a surprising variety of waterfowl—is the Andean, or "mountain," cat, a mysterious small feline.

A little larger than a house cat, the Andean cat is an elusive creature. Like many of the small cats of the Old World, it is almost never seen because of the remoteness of its home, its secretive nature, and—scientists believe —its extreme rarity.

As befits an animal inhabiting high altitudes, the Andean cat's coat is long and thick. Unlike most felines, its tail has hair of equal length all around. It is a rather attractive animal, silver-gray lined with orange spots above and a white speckled black below. Brown rings mark the tail. Most of what can be said of the Andean cat is supposition, for no one really knows how the cat lives and the animal has not been studied by scientists. Sharing the Andes with the Andean cat, although staying on the altiplano rather than the slopes, is a similar species, the pampas cat (*Felis pajeros*). It is a creature inhabiting wide-open expanses, highland and lowland, from Brazil and Ecuador to Bolivia, Peru, and Chile. Living in a habitat that is virtually treeless, the pampas cat is adapted to life on the ground. It moves rapidly on small feet in a manner that has been likened by zoologists to the graceful gait of a mongoose. The agility and speed of the pampas cat on the ground help it catch its prey—small creatures such as rodents, birds, small reptiles, and probably insects.

Over its extensive range, the pampas cat differs considerably in coloration. In the Andes, for instance, the cat is silver-gray with a red tinge, dotted on the flanks with red-brown spots. On the other hand, the pampas cat of the Mato Grosso, in southwestern Brazil, looks like an entirely different animal. It is yellowish brown with a black head, neck, and back and dark boots on the legs.

Whatever their coloration, unlike other smaller felines, most pampas cats can raise the long hairs that run down their backs until it forms a mane. The pampas cat raises its mane when it is agitated, a feature that is doubtless a protective adaptation because it makes the cat look much larger than it really is.

Open country is also the home of the kodkod (*Felis guigna*), a creature slightly larger than a housecat. Reddish-brown and speckled with black, this minim of a feline inhabits the coastal areas of Peru and Chile. It shuns areas where grassy vegetation dominates, since it needs some brush and trees for cover, but it does not venture into deep forest. The kodkod is a good climber and probably escapes aloft when in danger, but it seems to hunt its prey—small mammals—on the ground. Another midget feline is the little spotted cat (*Felis tigrina*), also known as the tiger cat. Creamy yellow, flecked with tiny black spots, this attractive little animal is restricted to tropical forests from Central through

South America. At home both on the ground and in the trees, the tiger cat hunts a variety of small animals, such as reptiles, rodents, birds, and insects.

Tiger cats, margays, and ocelots belong to a trio of yellow, black-spotted cats living in New World tropics and their fringes. A shade larger than the tiger cat (*Leopardus tigrinus*) is the margay (*Felis wiedii*), a superb climber that ranges from the Texas border country to southern Brazil and Bolivia. Margays dwell in both brush and, most frequently, in the forest. Because they have claws that are very long and sharp, and broad, elastic feet, these cats climb like acrobats. The margay can descend a tree or travel out on a limb head first. It can hang by its hind feet—even one hind foot—from a branch, pull itself from bough to bough with its front paws, and easily leap from limb to limb. Besides its elongated claws, the margay has another trait that contributes to its aerial nimbleness. For its size, its feet are much wider and far more flexible than those of other cats. Its hind feet, moreover, can rotate in a half circle, giving it the capacity to grip. This incredible ability to climb probably is an adaptation to hunting prey aloft. Although the margay has not been studied intensively in the wild, its diet probably is composed of arboreal animals, such as squirrels, tree rats, monkeys, and birds.

Resembling the margay and sharing much of the margay's range, although edging further south, is the ocelot (*Felis pardalis*). As large as a lynx, the ocelot is sometimes called the "painted leopard," because its pelt is dappled with black rosettes and stripes. Forest ocelots tend to be yellowish; those of more open areas are often grayish-white.

Ocelots inhabit both dry scrublands and forest, reaching their largest size in the South American jungle. Although lacking the margay's dexterity in trees, the ocelot is nevertheless a skillful climber. Ocelots living in the jungle prowl far up toward the canopy, both when hunting and in order to escape enemies, such as dogs. Unlike some of their New World relatives, ocelots are at least partly social. Pairs of these cats have been observed living together even out of mating season, sharing the hunt and their captured prey. When the cats are on the prowl, usually after dark, they communicate by calling back and forth to one another with vocalizations that resemble the sounds made by house cats. Ocelots eat a variety of small to medium-size animals, including anteaters, monkeys, squirrels, birds, lizards, and snakes.

The social life of ocelots also seems to include the sharing of parental responsibilities by both sexes. Ocelots breed at any time of year in the tropics but generally only during the spring farther north. They den in rocky clefts, under brush, or in hollow logs. Usually a litter has two young. In recent years, ocelots have declined in number, as have tiger cats and margays, since they have been hunted excessively for their pelts, which are highly prized in the fashion world. International conservation measures restricting trade in the pelts of rare cats have helped stem the decline due to the fur trade, but habitat destruction remains a serious threat to these creatures. Dry, rocky country studded with trees and shrubs is the home of the margay-size Geoffroy's cat (*Felis geoffroyi*). Ranging from northern Argentina to southern Bolivia, it favors habitat between deep forest and open plains. For the most part, its diet consists of small mammals, such as rodents and birds. This cat swims readily, however, and may therefore also feed on aquatic creatures.

Geoffroy's cats display surprising variability in color. Those living in the northern portion of the species' range are yellowish, sometimes yellow-brown. Southern Geoffroy's cats are silvery gray. All are speckled with fine spots, which are arranged in thin stripes on the face and neck.

No other small American cat is a better swimmer than the odd jaguarundi (*Felis yagouaroundi*), a short-legged, long-bodied cat a bit smaller than the ocelot. The jaguarundi, which has brown, black, gray, and red color phases, inhabits dense forest, chaparral, and swamps. The jaguarundi looks less like a feline than any other cat, resembling an otter or a large weasel. Its head is small, its body elongate, and its legs short. Primarily a ground animal, the jaguarundi's low-slung, narrow body enables it to thread its way with ease through thickets of brush and tangled vegetation.

When hunting, jaguarundis seek their prey on the ground as well as in the water. Fish and amphibians, in fact, furnish the water-loving jaguarundi with much of its diet. Jaguarundis living near agricultural areas do people a service by killing vast numbers of rats. In fact, tradition has it that before the coming of Europeans to the Americas, Indians tamed the mild-mannered jaguarundis and kept them as ratters.

Because it lacks the attractive coat of the ocelot and other spotted cats, the jaguarundi has not been hunted or trapped to excess. It remains common in many areas but is seldom seen because it prefers to go about its business in secrecy and stealth.

189. *Like a content house cat on a windowsill, Geoffroy's cat (Felis geoffroyi) spends hours resting on low branches in scrubby woodland and open bush country from southern Brazil to Argentina. This is one of several small South American cats whose life histories are largely blank pages. About 30 inches long from nose to tail tip, Geoffroy's cat has spotted fur that varies in color from reddish yellow to silvery gray. It is reported to be a nocturnal hunter, a skilled climber, and a willing swimmer.*

190, 192, *and* 194 *overleaves. A margay (Felis wiedii) confronts a collared anteater (Tamandua tetradactyla) on a branch in the South American rain forest and wisely retreats, for the cat would be no match for the arboreal anteater with its powerful arms and ripping foreclaws. The margay is found from the Rio Grande Valley in southernmost Texas to Brazil and Bolivia. It spends much of its life in trees, leaping from limb to limb, descending trunks headfirst, aided in its acrobatics by oversize feet and long claws. Like other small cats from the American tropics, the margay has been exploited ruthlessly for the fur trade and is considered an endangered species.*

196. *Horizontal rows of large spots account for the common name of the leopard cat (Felis bengalensis), a fierce nocturnal hunter that is known from Siberia to Southeast Asia and the Philippines, and west across India to Iran. In tropical forests, the leopard cat may be one of the most abundant four-footed predators, lurking near villages to feast on the rats and mice that thrive on man's crops and garbage and frequently making off with poultry.*

Small, Sleek, and Wily

Native to the tropics of the Old World—Eurasia and Africa—are a number of small to middle-size felines, many of them so mysterious they are seldom observed by scientists. Like other cats, they are wily, sleek, and superb hunters, and several count among the oddest felines alive.

One of these mysterious cats lives on the small island of Iriomote, which retains a deep and, in some areas, virgin forest within its rugged interior. Located at the southern tip of the Japanese archipelago just 120 miles from Taiwan, the island is known not only for its rare wild pigs and abundant bird life but also for a cat that is an evolutionary enigma. Prowling the forests on Iriomote, this feline (*Felis iriomotensis*) is so secretive that it was not discovered until 1965. The discovery of the Iriomote cat (*yamaneko*, in Japanese) sparked a controversy over its role in feline evolution that continues today. The cat, which is about a yard long—slightly larger than a domestic tabby—with a dark brown spotted coat, is extremely primitive, resembling an ancient cat that lived about four million years ago. Indeed, some Japanese scientists have proposed that it is almost a living replica of the forerunner of all cats, a living fossil that survived the ages unchanged on its remote island.

Although biologists tend to reject the suggestion that the Iriomote cat is really the ancestral feline, few deny that it is a true relic of the past. Among its primitive traits are external scent glands under the tail and the apparent ability to retract its claws. Parts of its skeleton mirror the bone structure of *Pseudalurus*, a fossil cat that probably hunted on the ground and that may be an important link in the feline evolutionary chain.

Some scientists suggest that the Iriomote cat is the ancestor of another small feline, the leopard cat (*Felis bengalensis*) of nearby southeastern Asia. The two are somewhat similar in appearance, although the leopard cat lacks the primitive traits of the Iriomote species. Perhaps in the very distant past, a cat of the Iriomote type once roved not only the island but the mainland as well, and there gradually differentiated into the present form of the leopard cat.

The Iriomote cat probably breeds from December to April and has up to three kittens. So far, however, no one has been able to observe a mother with young. A few Iriomote cats have been kept in captivity, and based on what has been observed in these specimens, the cats probably live only about ten years in the wild.

There may be fewer than one hundred cats remaining on the island, and some conservationists fear for the animal's future. Biologists estimate that a single cat requires almost 700 acres of forest as its territory. The forests prowled by the cat are being disrupted by development, and pesticides have decreased the feline's prey.

Another mysterious feline is the bay cat (*Felis badia*) of Borneo. It is listed in scientific literature describing the feline tribe, but almost all else about it other than its description—golden red in color and about the size of a European wildcat—is unreported.

Something of how the bay cat lives, however, can be deduced from the lives of its close relatives, the golden cats of Africa and Asia (*Felis aurata* and *Felis temmincki*). The African species, which is close to a bobcat in size, inhabits the deep rain forests that stretch across the midsection of the continent. Slim-legged, graceful animals, they seem to hunt both on the ground and in the trees. The slightly smaller Temminck's golden cat of southern Asia is similarly a forest animal that is as much at home on the ground as in the trees. This Asian cat is a rugged predator, feeding on animals ranging in size from hares to buffalo calves.

Another denizen of Africa and Asia is the jungle cat (*Felis chaus*). In Africa, it inhabits the muddy wetlands of the Nile delta. In Asia, it lives chiefly from Asia Minor east to India and Burma. Jungle cats of temperate areas breed in the late winter or, at the northern edge of their range, in early spring. Abandoned burrows of other animals or crevices in rocks provide a nursery for the kits, which may number from two to six. The male helps his mate rear the young.

The flat-headed cat (*Felis planiceps*) of Southeast Asia

and Borneo seems to prey on fish, frogs, and other small aquatic creatures. Although rarely seen in its native forests, there are several reasons to suspect that the flat-headed cat's diet is at least partially piscatory. In captivity, it has greedily accepted live fish. Also, teeth that are missing or small and rather blunt in most other cats are large and very sharp in the flat-headed cat, which as its name implies has a skull that is flattened and an elongated muzzle; this trait is obviously helpful in seizing and holding squirmy victims. This cat, about the size of a serval, also inhabits wet areas, such as swamps and stream edges in the jungle.

Like the flat-headed cat, the fishing cat (*Felis viverrinus*) is a southern Asian feline that has seldom been studied in the wild. It seems to stalk small animals of the water, although, despite its name, it also kills mammals. Bobcat-size and as feisty as a wildcat, the fishing cat haunts the water's edge around marshes, swamps, rivers, and mangroves that grow along the coasts. As one might expect from a creature that hunts around water, the fishing cat is a superb swimmer.

The leopard cats (*Felis bengalensis*), two types of which range from northern China to Java, are also excellent swimmers, although they are not fishers. Inhabitants of both brush and forest, from sea level to high mountains, leopard cats are similar to flat-headed cats but resemble tabby-size leopards. In appearance graceful, even delicate, they are in fact courageous and ferocious. For their size they are bruisers—tough, vicious, and savage. Leopard cats sometimes kill animals many times their weight, such as the young of small deer. For the most part, however, they subsist on creatures such as rodents, birds, and even bats. They climb with incredible agility, exhibit superb balance on tree branches, and readily search through the forest canopy looking for prey.

Even smaller than the leopard cats, which are their close cousins, are the rusty-spotted cats (*Felis rubiginosus*) of southern India and Sri Lanka. They exist in a wide range of habitats, from dry plains to humid jungles. Prowling by night, these little cats hunt for rodents and other small mammals and birds.

Southeast Asia is the home of another small spotted feline, the marbled cat (*Felis marmorata*), a rare, secretive animal that always seems to arch its back when still, whether sitting or standing, a behavioral trait no one has fathomed. Although it climbs with ease, this cat hunts mostly on the forest floor, stalking small mammals and birds. Marbled cats, which have a gray coat with dark marbling, show a tolerance to a wide variety of climatic conditions; they range from the forests of Borneo and Burma into the Himalayan Mountains.

The cold, windswept mountains and high steppes of central Asia are the home of the Pallas's cat (*Felis manul*). From the southern fringes of Siberia south to the Himalayans, the Pallas's cat roves country as high as 12,000 feet above sea level, areas that are bitter cold in winter and sun-baked and dry in summer. Not graceful in appearance, the Pallas's cat is built to survive the cold. The length of an ordinary housecat, it is much heavier, the extra bulk producing more body heat and thus helping it keep warm. Its extremities and ears are short, another adaptation to living in subarctic weather (the blood loses little heat when circulating to the extremities because it does not have to travel far). Along its flanks and underside, the Pallas's cat sports luxuriant fur, which insulates the creature against cold and snow. Because the fur on its back is close-cropped, it can absorb solar heat quickly.

Largest of the small to middle-size Old World felines is one that from an evolutionary standpoint is as interesting as the cat of Iriomote Island. The clouded leopard (*Neofelis nebulosa*), in the view of many scientists, links the big cats with their smaller relatives, since it has characteristics of both. Its teeth and skull are similar to those of a big cat, while its other bodily traits are like those of the smaller felines.

Shy, nocturnal, keeping to the most inaccessible areas, the clouded leopard almost qualifies as an arboreal animal. So short-legged that it can look almost inept on the ground, the clouded leopard is the size of a lynx but has a longer body. It rambles through the trees of southern Asia's jungles with a verve and ease perhaps equaled by no other cat. While this cat sometimes hunts on the ground, it is most often found in trees. Leaping, creeping, even hanging from branches by its paws, the clouded leopard snares monkeys, birds, and other arboreal animals in their lofty homes. It also kills ground animals as large as deer and wild pigs, sometimes by leaping on them from above, other times by springing from ambush.

The clouded leopard—like the snow leopard, not a true leopard at all—ranges from Nepal and Burma to Indochina, southern China, and Taiwan, not far from Iriomote Island. It has been frequently kept in captivity, but, as is the case with so many wild cats, much about its natural behavior is unknown.

201; 202 *and* 204 *overleaves. The jungle cat* (Felis chaus) *seems misnamed, for it prefers damp habitats—swamps and marshes, the reedy borders of lakes and streams—and frogs far outweigh typical feline food in its diet. The jungle cat reaches the African continent at the Nile delta of Egypt, but otherwise it is strictly an Asiatic species, ranging from the Caspian Sea to India and Burma. The jungle cat's coat is a muddy tan, its ears pointed, its legs long for running down prey. At times jungle cats will venture onto drier grasslands, hunting such birds as doves plus hares and other small animals. And they have been known to take up residence in abandoned buildings where mice run rampant. Unlike most other wild cats, the male jungle cat helps raise the three to five kittens.*

206 *overleaf. Little is known about the behavior of the marbled cat* (Felis marmorata). *It surely is one of the prettiest small cats; a coat splashed with irregular spots and dots suggests a clouded leopard in miniature. It may also be among the rarest, for its Asiatic forest haunts from Nepal to Burma and Borneo are being systematically and rapidly destroyed. Secretive, nocturnal, and arboreal, the marbled cat is rarely observed in the wild and may vanish before we come to understand it.*

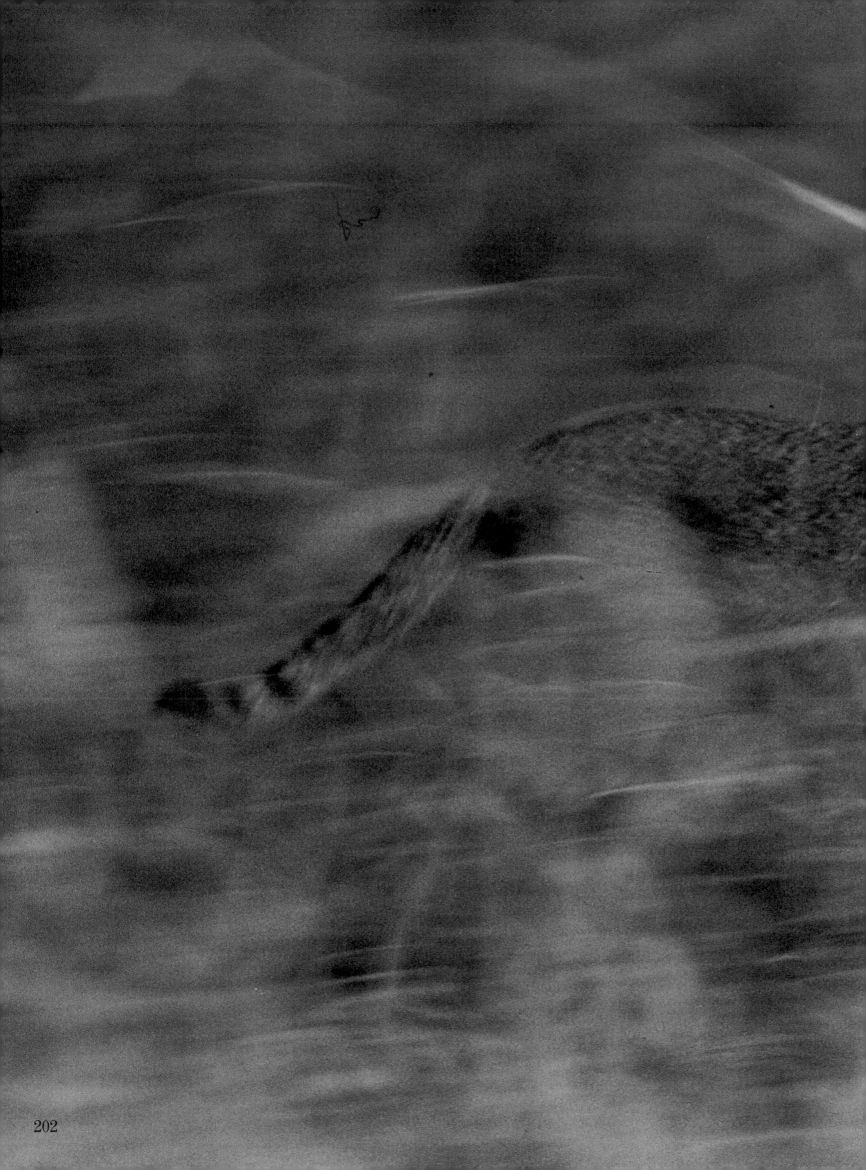

208 *and* **209; 210** *overleaf. Another water-loving feline from Asia is the aptly named fishing cat (Felis viverrinus). Crouched on a slick rock or sandbar, or wading in the shallows, it scoops out fish with forepaws on which the claws do not retract into sheaths. And as befits its life-style, there are webs between its toes. The fishing cat is found from India to China to Java; the size of a bobcat, its haunts are mangrove tangles, tidal marshes, and river deltas. An excellent and willing swimmer, the fishing cat augments its diet with crabs, frogs, snakes, and mollusks.*

212. *Largest feline on earth, the tiger (Panthera tigris) is a beast of extraordinary beauty and awesome strength, a predator without rival among terrestrial animals whose name alone can strike fear in man. A 10-foot male Bengal tiger from India will weigh as much as 600 pounds; a Siberian tiger might measure 13 feet from nose to tip of tail and weigh 700 pounds! Contemporary scientists recognize six other subspecies: the Caspian tiger, Chinese tiger, Indochinese tiger, and three island-isolated races on Java, Sumatra, and Bali. The Bali tiger likely is extinct, and others may soon follow.*

Fearful Symmetry

The gently sloping clearing in a Thai jungle is bathed in the morning sun, which has just risen above the crest of a grassy incline. Scattered about the slope, which rises from a valley covered by forest, graze sambar deer, dark brown forms silhouetted against the soft green hues of the grass. The scene is peaceful, without a hint of the tension with which deer and other prey animals often live. Suddenly, one of the deer lifts its head and sniffs the air. Within moments, another follows suit. Soon the entire herd is alert and taut, prepared to flee at an instant's notice.

From the dense forest at the base of the slope, muntjacs, the so-called barking deer, utter their sharp yaps of warning. Their cries cut through the quiet of the morning. Large and small creatures alike have sensed danger afoot—danger in the form of a lithe, powerful striped cat, Asia's dominant predator, the tiger (*Panthera tigris*).

Camouflaged by a patch of forest, the tiger is out of sight, but its progress and direction of travel can be measured by the barking of the muntjacs. The cat is heading for the clearing. A few minutes pass, and then, silent as a wraith, the tiger emerges from the trees, moving at a leisurely but rapid pace, head held below its massive shoulders, tail drooping gracefully behind. The sambar watches intently as the tiger travels up the slope, several hundred yards from the nearest deer in the herd. Sambar are a natural prey of the tiger, but in this instance the great cat pays them scant attention. It is obviously not hungry and on a mission of some sort that the human mind could never fathom. As the tiger nears the crest of the slope, it pauses for a few seconds, then turns its huge head back toward the way it came. Its amber eyes survey the land like a ruler overlooking its realm, eyes that are calm but terrible, bespeaking a fearful strength encased in a body of exquisite design and symmetry of muscle.

Largest of the cats, the tiger epitomizes the beauty and brutal power of nature. Thickly built, it has a long body, a thick, short neck, and sturdy, powerful legs built for stalking, not swift running. Its shoulders and back are broad and ripple with steely muscles.

Tigers vary in size according to subspecies. The type that gives this striped hunter the title of the biggest cat lives in northern Asia. Called the Siberian tiger (*Panthera tigris altaica*), it may surpass 600 pounds and be more than a dozen feet in length. The tiger's gorgeous stripes, the pattern of which enables the cat to blend marvelously with the shadows and sunlight of the forest, is unique among felines. Moreover, its ferocity is legendary. Tigers will attack animals as large as elephants and rhinoceroses. And while all of the great cats occasionally prey on our species, none has done it with such frequency and savagery as the tiger, although its reputation is far worse than its actual deeds.

The tiger's reputation as a killer of people is one of the factors that has led to its decline, a decrease in numbers that has eradicated many subspecies of tigers and has endangered the entire species. Fearing tigers, people who share the countryside with them have killed them without compunction, sometimes with good reason. Tigers also have been slaughtered for their pelts, which, until laws were passed to prevent trade in tiger hides, were a staple of high-fashion furs.

The worst pressure on the tiger, however, is from the destruction of its habitat. Tigers, particularly in southern Asia, live in some of the most densely populated areas on earth. As people have proliferated, in poverty and without exercising environmental common sense, the land has been degraded, the game on which the tiger depends depleted, and the cats simply crowded out of their ancient havens. A predator that once roamed over a vast portion of the world and numbered in the scores of thousands now has been reduced to a few pitiful remnants holding out in a sea of humanity.

Tigers once ranged across Asia from the northern Middle East to Korea, and from Siberia to Java and Bali. While most of the world's tigers inhabit warm regions, the tiger may not be tropical in origin. Some scientists believe that tigers evolved in northern Asia, perhaps even on the fringes of the Arctic. Possibly during prehistory, as the great herds of big-game animals that roved the north dwindled, tigers moved to new hunting grounds in the south. Some migrated west toward southern Russia and Turkey, others east to the Orient or south toward India and Indochina. Great, shaggy tigers still haunt the cold conifer forests of Manchuria and Siberia, evoking images of the vanished Pleistocene Ice Age as they pad through the snow.

The tiger is a creature that primarily inhabits forested regions; in fact, almost any type of Asian woodland can support tigers. In China, tigers have roved oak and pine forests. In Turkey, Iran, and southern Russia, the cats have prowled woodlands of tamarisk interspersed with marshes. Indian tigers have been at home in forests of dry thorn and tropical evergreens. Southeast Asian rain forests are prime tiger habitat. On the northeast coast of India and in Sumatra, tigers have found a haven in swamps of tangled mangrove trees. In such places, the cats sometimes live semi-aquatically, often swimming for miles from island to island.

Tigers tolerate a wide variety of altitudinal extremes. They range from sea level to the heights of Asia. The great cats have been observed as high as 13,000 feet in the Himalayas, although they live mostly at lower altitudes. As befits a creature that seems to have evolved in the northlands, tigers can withstand severe winter temperatures. Areas where they live in northern Asia regularly experience temperatures as low as 30 degrees Fahrenheit below zero in winter.

Most areas that once had tiger populations, however, have them no longer. Once common in the jungled hills of Bali, adding to its mystique, the Bali tiger (*Panthera tigris balica*), which is relatively small and light in color, seems to have slipped into extinction. Just west of Bali, on Java, a handful of that island's tigers (*Panthera tigris sondaica*) remain, and their survival is in doubt. Similarly, Sumatran and Chinese tigers (*Panthera tigris sumatrae* and *Panthera tigris amoyensis*) are in serious danger of vanishing. The tigers (*Panthera tigris virgata*) that roved the mountains and steppes around the Caspian sea are seldom seen, perhaps gone from Iran and southern Russia and possibly surviving as only a few isolated individuals in remote parts of Afghanistan. The Siberian tiger (*Panthera tigris altaica*) numbers only a few hundred in the wild. The tigers of Indochina (*Panthera tigris corbetti*) and the "Bengal" tiger (*Panthera tigris tigris*) of the Indian subcontinent survive, but even they are in danger. As of the late 1970s, possibly four or five thousand tigers of these two types remained, while a half century ago the subcontinent alone had 40,000 of these cats.

However, there are signs that with human help the tiger may yet survive. As a result of a worldwide effort to amass funds to support tiger conservation, and due to intensive studies of tigers' interaction with their environment, other animals, and people, tigers in India and in some adjacent nations seem to be holding their own and even making a modest comeback. If this trend continues, the cause of wildlife conservation will have achieved a remarkable victory that holds future promise for other endangered species.

By the early 1980s, scientists estimated the number of tigers in the region of the Indian subcontinent to be 7,000. One of the reasons for this encouraging and surprising increase is the establishment of tiger reserves, vast areas partially covered with forest from which disruption by humans has been eliminated or at least pared to a bare minimum. India now has almost a dozen such reserves, from Periyar at the foot of the subcontinent to Manas in the hill country of Assan, near the country's northern border with Bhutan. Some are new; others were established in existing national parks. The reserves have undeniably helped, although none of them contain the immense tracts of unbroken forest needed by a breeding population of tigers to maintain a genetically diversified stock in a given area. To prevent inbreeding, a reproducing population of tigers must number between 200 and 300 animals. The amount of land required to support this number of tigers is a minimum of 800 square miles, and some scientists believe it is more than twice that area.

Unlike lions, tigers live most of their lives in solitary fashion, although they have more social interaction than scientists once suspected. Researchers have found that two or more adults sometimes come together when one of them has made a kill, and they may share a meal amicably. Mostly, however, tigers roam their territories alone, staying out of one another's way.

The large size of the territory required by a solitary male means that home ranges of tigers often overlap. Sometimes more than one male will share a portion of territory, but often they will contend with one another for hunting rights to a particular area, especially when the overlapping area is the center of a tiger's territory. Even though a tiger may claim a large area, it concentrates its activities in one part—where game and water are abundant, for instance. Such an area will be defended more vigorously than fringe areas.

Scientists believe that the territory of one male tiger generally overlaps those of several females. Overlapping territories enable male and female to encounter one another for the purposes of mating. The male ruler of a territory may mate with several or all of the females who share areas with him. Over several years, the same male and female may meet each mating season and, although by no means monogamous or a family, produce several litters of young.

Males and females find one another by scent as well as by calling. Tigers regularly mark their territories by spraying vegetation with urine and also by marking it with a secretion from their anal glands. Like cougars, they scratch scrapes into the ground and deposit their droppings on them.

Tigers have several different calls. Two tigers meeting amicably will produce a sound technically known as prusten but also called chuffling, which describes the noise aptly. The sound is made as the cat expels air through its nostrils and partly closed lips. Zoo tigers that gain a fondness for their keeper sometimes chuffle when he or she approaches. Some zoo people have themselves learned to chuffle using this technique to evoke the same response from their cats.

Tigers also woof, grunt, and roar. Although roaring takes place at a variety of times, tigers seem to use it as a means of communication during the mating season. The cats also roar repeatedly during the mating act itself.

A female who is ready to mate is sometimes followed by several males, perhaps as many as a half dozen. She may mate with a number of them or with just one. Male tigers sometimes battle fiercely for the rights to a female. Although these fights usually do not end in the death of one of the contestants, they can be bloody affairs, with males ripping and biting one another and causing the forest to tremble with their roars. Mating completed, the father takes no part in rearing the young, although sometimes male and female remain with each other for a week or two before they separate, each going their own way.

Heavy brush, a rock shelter, or a cave can serve as the den in which the female gives birth to her young, about the same number per litter as lions deliver. The four to nine newborn cubs weigh two or three pounds each, but within two months, at the time they can leave the den with their mother, they reach at least ten pounds in weight. By then they are also able to eat meat, although they are not fully weaned.

Soon after the cubs first leave the den they desert it

altogether, and the tiger family takes to roving the countryside. At first, the mother is solely responsible for feeding her family, but as the cubs complete their first year of life, they start to hunt on their own.

At one year of age, the cubs are larger than the average cougar or leopard and are capable of downing medium-size prey, such as wild pigs, but they still have difficulty with larger beasts. By the end of their second year, however, the young have reached full size and, capable of living on their own, gradually break their family ties and wander off in the forest.

Tigers need forest, because it is the habitat of the large herbivores that are their chief prey, although they also eat many other creatures including crocodiles, turtles, fish, rodents, and ground birds. Water buffalo, adult and young deer, massive nilgai antelope, wild swine, and sometimes even young elephants furnish the tiger with the most important part of its diet.

The tiger stalks its larger prey by night. Using its keen eyes and ears, it patrols its hunting territory, slipping along watercourses, ravines, and jungle trails. Moving at between two and three miles an hour, a tiger on the prowl for food may travel more than thirty miles between dusk and dawn if it does not find a victim before sunrise. Although it has endurance for long-distance travel, the tiger is not a sprinter; therefore, like the lion, it needs to stalk close to its victim, then strike with a sudden rush. A target that is totally oblivious to the tiger's presence can be taken by the cat from a distance of slightly less than thirty yards. If the prey senses danger, however, it may dash away. As a result, the cat must get within a few yards before revealing itself or it will likely lose its meal.

The tiger does not need heavy vegetation for a successful strike. So adept is this huge cat at stalking that it can move unseen through vegetation that seems hardly dense enough to hide a tabby. More often than not, the tiger rushes its victim from behind or from the flank. Like a thunderbolt, the cat leaps upon its prey, sometimes atop its back. Raking with its claws, the tiger bites the victim in the neck, especially the throat, and thrusts it to the ground. Other times, the cat keeps its hind feet on the ground and rears up on the unfortunate creature it has attacked. Occasionally, the tiger may try to bring an animal to the ground by biting it in the leg, then flipping it over. The kill almost always follows a neck bite. If this bite does not dispatch the victim outright, death results by strangulation.

The tiger does not begin to eat as soon as it has killed.

Instead, it carries its prey—even animals as large as water buffalo—to a secluded place. Tigers regularly carry victims almost as large as they are for several hundred feet. Depending on the size of the prey, it may last the cat for several days. Tigers eat until they are stuffed, which can take an hour or so. Scientists who have watched tigers on their kills say that in one day a tiger can consume more than 300 pounds of meat, though at several sittings. Between sittings, a tiger may first cover up the partially eaten carcass and then wander, drink water, or sleep, but once hunger returns, it resumes feeding.

Scientists who study tigers to determine how they interact with other predators in reserves found that, in some thickly forested areas at least, tigers can share territory with leopards because of the striped cats' preference for larger prey. Leopards eat creatures such as small or young deer. Tigers at times take small species and the young of larger species, but they also feed on much larger prey such as full-grown sambar, which are almost as big as American elks. Heavy vegetation, moreover, enables leopards to keep out of the way of the more powerful tigers. Despite their size and ferocity, tigers sometimes end up on the losing end of the battle when they attack large animals, such as gaur. This big wild ox has fatally gored and trampled tigers. The wild boar sometimes also emerges on the winning side of a confrontation.

Tigers also may become the prey. Crocodiles occasionally kill a tiger in the water, while hyenas take unattended young. And the Indian wild dog, or dhole, will attack a tiger, often to drive it away from its victim. One dog is certainly no match for the cat but dholes run in large packs, which beset their opponent from all sides.

A tiger surrounded by dholes is caught in the center of a cyclone of ever-moving, darting, snapping savagery. The cat may use its mighty paws to batter several of the dogs to smithereens but still they attack. Frustrated, the tiger may try to run but it is no match for the speed of the dholes. They pursue, biting at the tiger from all sides. If there are enough dogs to prevent the tiger's escape it may be killed.

The tiger's most important interaction with another species, however, is its contact with humans. Humans teem around many of the reserves where tigers survive, and these powerful cats can threaten not only human life but also human livelihood. Especially when their natural prey is scarce, tigers readily kill cattle and other livestock, which are critically important to the impoverished people who live in the vicinity of most tiger areas. As for human life, most tigers do not prey on people, but some do. To determine why, scientists have studied the relationship between the cats and people in an area notorious for its "man-eating" tigers, the Sundarbans Delta.

Historically, the tigers of the Sundarbans have taken a grisly toll of human lives. Even within recent years, more than 100 people of the region have died due to attacks by tigers. Many residents of the area, which includes a major tiger reserve, have demanded that the Indian government halt its tiger conservation programs. Studies of the problem in the Sundarbans has shown, however, that only 3 percent of the cats in the delta deliberately stalk, kill, and eat people. Other tigers of the region may be aggressive and attack people if startled, but they do not hunt them regularly. Many of these accidents occurred when people ventured into the forest to cut firewood and lumber, or to search for wild honey, and blundered into the cats. Much forestry work goes on during the time of year when tigers have cubs and are especially defensive.

A good portion of human fatalities caused by tigers throughout India, in fact, seems to be when people enter a tiger habitat to find wood or food. Since much of the area outside the reserves has been denuded of timber, however, the tiger's refuge may be the only place where people can find the necessities of daily life.

Conservationists say the conflicts between tigers and people can be reduced by sound environmental planning and forestry practices outside reserves and by teaching people how to avoid confrontations with the big cats. In the long run, improving the habitat for the tiger could improve the environment for people, raising their living standards and quality of life.

The problems that must be solved are complex and difficult, but if the tiger can be saved, so, by example, can other species of wild creatures whose interests do not always coincide with those of people. The price tag will be high, especially for the developing countries in which most tigers live. However, anyone who treasures the spirit of the wild and takes heart from its continued presence can thrill to the fact that, in a few last places, the tiger still roams free.

221. *A Bengal tiger* (Panthera tigris tigris) *surveys its domain— India's Ranthambhor National Park. The tiger's vertical stripes are unique in the cat world, but the pattern and background color of the coat will vary from race to race. For example, the coat of a Bengal tiger commonly is bright yellow-brown. In contrast, the rare Javan tiger* (P. tigris sondaica) *has a dark red coat with thin stripes. But like the Bali tiger* (P. tigris balica), *smallest of all the subspecies, it too may have passed into the void of extinction. At most, a half a dozen individuals still survive on the 650-mile-long island in the Indian Ocean.*

224 *overleaf. A Bengal tiger stalks a herd of alert chital in Ranthambhor National Park. Deer and wild cattle—gaur and nilgai—are the principal prey of Indian tigers. The Siberian tiger* (P. tigris altaica), *largest of the clan, hunts wild boars, elk, moose, and even the dangerous brown bear.*

226 *overleaf. In hot pursuit of a sambar deer, a Bengal tiger will drag its victim to the ground, then seize the throat in a strangling grip.*

228 *overleaf. The water of an Indian marsh sprays wildly as a tiger splashes after a hapless sambar calf.*

222 *and* 223. *In the flickering shadows of dense forest or the faded grass by a marsh, the tiger's stripes hide hunter from the hunted. But the tiger's exquisitely designed coat has not provided the grandest of wild cats with protection from its only enemy, man. A century ago, the Bengal tiger numbered in the tens of thousands. But relentless slaughter for sport—as many as 40 tigers might have been shot on a single safari—and later, the fur trade, reduced the population in India to fewer than 2,000 in the 1970s. The establishment of several reserves, however, has led to a modest comeback.*

230 *above. Its jaws still clamped on its victim's neck, a Bengal tiger drags a sambar deer out of the shallows. Tigers invariably carry their prey to dense cover, then begin their feast at the choicest part of the carcass, the rump.*

230 *below. With little effort, a Bengal tiger hauls its prey to hiding. Full-grown animals weighing more than 400 pounds will be dragged the length of a football field from the scene of a kill.*

231. *This freshly killed sambar may be shared with other adult tigers in the vicinity, but there will be no catfight over the carcass. They will wait until the successful hunter has eaten his or her fill.*

232 *overleaf. Satiated after having eaten 50 pounds of meat in one meal, a Bengal tiger rests by the half-consumed carcass of a sambar. Covering the remains with grass and dirt, the tiger will return to feed until every scrap, even the skin and hooves, is utilized.*

234. *A satisfying feast triggers a mighty yawn that reveals three-inch long fangs. A full-grown tiger will consume three tons of meat in a year, and the biggest of big cats, is an opportunist that will eat anything it can catch—wild ungulates and livestock for the most part, but also fish, frogs, turtles, birds, locusts, and more than infrequently, humans. While the tiger's reputation as a man-killer has been exaggerated, the cat certainly can be blamed for more human deaths than any other mammal. For example, tigers killed 129 people near the mouth of the Ganges River in a three-year span.*

236 *overleaf. A tigress approaches a stream-bank with two well-grown cubs, most likely females. Young males leave the family group early, when they are a year old. Lacking hunting skills, they risk fatal encounters with dangerous prey, including porcupines that leave the cat with a crippling jawful of quills. If it survives those formative years, and avoids man's guns, poisons, and traps, a tiger might live for twenty-five years in the wild.*

235. *White tigers occasionally occur in the wild, born into otherwise normal litters. These partial albinos are mutants, with ice-blue eyes, eggshell-white fur, and gray-brown stripes. Their unusual coloration makes them conspicuous, and almost invariably they fall victim to predators. In captivity, lines of white tigers have been bred successfully.*

238 *and* **239.** *In the sweltering forests of India and Southeast Asia, tigers may spend midday hours partly submerged in cool ponds and rivers. Sumatran tigers* (P. tigris sumatrae) *often swim several miles from one coastal island to another. Tigers are protected by law on Sumatra, but illegal hunting continues—a skin is worth several thousand dollars— and the population has declined below 1,000 individuals. On the mainland to the north, the Indochinese tiger* (P. tigris corbetti), *found from Burma to Vietnam and the Malay Peninsula, may actually have increased in number, its food supply augmented by the victims of continuing strife in the region.*

240 *overleaf. The massive Siberian tiger, many scientists believe, was the progenitor of all races of* Panthera tigris. *From its origins in cold northeast Asia, the tiger spread outward in two arms— south into the tropical forests and to the East Indian islands, and west as far as Turkey. The latter race, the Caspian tiger* (P. tigris virgata) *hangs on today by a thread. A dozen or two tigers may survive in the most remote parts of Iran and Afghanistan. Also near extinction is the Chinese tiger* (P. tigris amoyensis). *The Yangtze Valley is its last stronghold.*

242 and **243.** *Siberian tigers frolic in the snow. Fewer than 400 of their kind exist in the wild today in China, North Korea, and in the Soviet Union, where the tiger has begun to recover under government protection. In contrast, more than 1,000 Siberian tigers are kept in zoos around the world—a gene pool that could assure the survival of the species.*

244 and **245; 246** overleaf. The Siberian tiger's long winter coat is an adaptation to the harsh climate of its homeland. Modern, farsighted zoos are devoting their efforts to captive breeding of endangered mammals, including the Asiatic lion and snow leopard. Captive collections will be carefully managed, with animal exchanges arranged between zoos to assure successful propagation. Thus if conservation efforts in the Soviet Union fail, the zoos will be the last refuge for the Siberian tiger. But for several races of Panthera tigris, it is too late. At least 250 animals, biologists say, are needed to assure a sound genetic blend.

The National Audubon Society is among the oldest and largest private conservation organizations in the world. With over 515,000 members and more than 500 local chapters across the country, the Society works in behalf of our natural heritage through environmental education and conservation action. It protects wildlife in more than seventy sanctuaries from coast to coast. It also operates outdoor education centers and ecology workshops and publishes the prizewinning AUDUBON magazine, AMERICAN BIRDS magazine, newsletters, films, and other educational materials. For further information regarding membership in the Society, write to the National Audubon Society, 950 Third Avenue, New York, New York 10022.

Notes on Photographers

Alain Aigouin is an amateur photographer living in the south of France. His work has appeared in a number of French publications.

Rod Allin is a staff cinematographer for the *Wild Kingdom* television program and a professional wildlife photographer.

Yann Arthus-Bertrand, a French photographer, lived and worked in Kenya for three years. His work has been published in magazines such as *Geo* and he is the author of six books, including *Lion*.

Joan Baron specializes in photographing wild and domestic animals. She travels regularly to Africa to photograph animals in reserves and her work has been widely published; her large-format prints hang in hundreds of private collections. She is also the author of three illustrated books on domestic cats.

Erwin and Peggy Bauer are writers and photographers living in Jackson Hole, Wyoming. For thirty-five years their work has appeared in such publications as *Audubon*, *National Geographic*, and *Outdoor Life*. They have written and illustrated over a dozen books, most recently, *Photographing the West*.

Wolfgang Bayer was born in Austria, where he studied engineering, and now lives in Wyoming. He has photographed and directed more than 125 wildlife documentaries for PBS, the National Geographic Society, and *Wide World of Animals*.

Stanley Breeden, a native of Australia, now lives near New Delhi, India. He has photographed wildlife throughout the world. His work appeared in *The Audubon Society Book of Wild Animals* and he has also written and photographed wildlife documentaries, including *Land of the Tiger* for the National Geographic Society.

Stewart Cassidy is a professional photographer specializing in the wildlife of the Rocky Mountains. His work has taken him to East Africa, Antarctica, South America, Australia, and China.

W. Perry Conway has been a wildlife photographer for ten years. His Colorado-based company produces educational natural history presentations.

Jack Couffer is a cinematographer whose credits include Walt Disney's True Life Series and *Jonathan Livingston Seagull*, for which he was nominated for an Academy Award.

Raimund Cramm is a German technician and award-winning wildlife photographer. He has photographed on four continents and his work has appeared in many publications.

Edward R. Degginger, a retired research chemist, has been a freelance photographer for more than twenty years. His primary interest is natural history. His photographs have been published in books, magazines, and encyclopedias.

Phil Degginger is a professional photographer whose subjects include travel and industry, as well as the natural and physical sciences.

Fulvio Eccardi is an Italian photographer and a director of documentary films. He holds a degree in biology.

Jean-Paul Ferrero was born in France and now lives in the United States. Some 4,000 of his photographs have been published, appearing in periodicals and books throughout the world, including *The Audubon Society Book of Trees.*

Maurice Fievet, a painter and photographer, works principally in Africa. His work has been published in France and throughout the world.

Jeff Foott has been a marine biologist, a mountain climbing guide, a member of the National Ski Patrol, and a National Park Ranger, as well as a wildlife photographer and filmmaker. His pictures of wildlife have appeared in leading natural history magazines including *Audubon* and *National Geographic.*

Warren Garst, a trained zoologist, has been the chief wildlife cinematographer for the *Wild Kingdom* television program since its inception.

François Gohier is a French writer and photographer who specializes in the wildlife of South America. His photographs have also appeared in *The Audubon Society Book of Insects.*

Peter Johnson lives in South Africa and travels throughout the continent studying and photographing wildlife. Recent books in which his work appears include *Antarctica* and *Okavango.*

Stephen J. Krasemann, a nature photographer whose work appears regularly in many natural history publications, is a contract photographer for *National Geographic.*

Jean-Michel Labat is a French photographer whose work has appeared in the national and international press and in a number of scholarly books.

Michael Leach is a British photographer and the director of a small film company.

Pat and Tom Leeson specialize in photographing the wildlife of the western United States. Their work has appeared in natural history publications such as *Audubon* and *National Geographic,* as well as a number of books.

Tom McHugh is a professional cinematographer who began his career working for Walt Disney Productions. In recent years, he has concentrated on still photography.

L. David Mech, a wildlife research biologist for the U.S. Fish and Wildlife Service, has studied the behavior of carnivores—principally the wolf—since 1958.

Gary Milburn has been a wildlife photographer for more than twelve years. Formerly he was an aquatic biologist with the Environmental Protection Agency.

C. Allan Morgan lives in Tucson, Arizona, and specializes in desert and marine still photography. His work has appeared in *Audubon, Natural History,* and *Ranger Rick* magazines.

Nadine Orobona is a Los Angeles-based photographer. She is the author of *The Photographer's Computer Handbook,* published in 1984.

Klaus Paysan is a German photographer with a particular interest in the peoples and animals of Africa. His photographs are regularly published in wildlife books and magazines.

John Pearson was a British pilot for East Africa Airways. In 1953 he moved to Kenya where he worked as a professional still photographer and cinematographer until his death in 1978.

E. Hanumantha Rao lives in Bangalore, India. His photographs of Indian wildlife have been reproduced worldwide.

Mitch Reardon lives and works in South Africa. With Margaux Reardon, he has written two books, *Etosha* and *Zululand;* both are illustrated with his photographs.

Hans Reinhard lives on a small farm outside of Heidelberg with his family and a host of wild animals. He is author of *Die Technik der Wildphotografie.*

Gerald Rilling spent twelve years teaching secondary school in Africa and working with Jane Goodall at the Gombe Stream Research Center. He lives in Rockford, Illinois, and travels to Africa whenever possible.

Jacques Robert, a dentist in France, has recently extended his talents into the field of professional photography. His work has appeared in French and international publications.

Galen Rowell is both a photojournalist and a mountaineer. His photographs have appeared in numerous publications, including *National Geographic* and *International Wildlife*. He is the author of six books, among them *High and Wild* and *Mountains of the Middle Kingdom*.

Leonard Lee Rue III lives in the Delaware Water Gap area of New Jersey. His photographs appear regularly in such magazines as *Audubon*, *Natural History*, and *Newsweek*. He is also the author of eighteen books.

Len Rue, Jr. is a full-time wildlife photographer. He lives in New Jersey where he teaches a course on wildlife photography and conducts photographic seminars with his father, Leonard Lee Rue III.

Sylvia Howe Thompson, a student and lecturer in biological anthropology, has conducted research in Africa and India, and is currently researching mother-infant relationships in primates. She has been interested in photography and filmmaking since high school.

R. Van Nostrand, formerly the staff photographer for the San Diego Zoo, is a regular contributor to *San Diego Zoonooz* magazine and an active photo-lecturer. His photographs of wildlife have been widely published.

Jean-Phillipe Varin is a French biologist and photographer. He founded Jacana, the well-known international nature photography agency, and is co-author of *Photographing Wildlife*.

Albert Visage was an electrical engineer before becoming a full-time wildlife photographer.

Belinda Wright, a wildlife filmmaker and photographer, lives in India. With her husband, Stanley Breeden, she filmed the 1985 National Geographic documentary *Land of the Tiger*. Her work has appeared in many publications, including *The Audubon Society Book of Wild Animals*.

Gregory A. Yovan lives in Connecticut. He specializes in photographing the wildlife of the northeastern United States.

Guenter Ziesler has photographed the wildlife of South America, the Galapagos Islands, New Guinea, Africa, and India, as well as his native Europe. He has recently published *Safari: The East African Diaries of a Wildlife Photographer*.

Photo Credits

Lord of the Savannas
Yann Arthus-Bertrand/Jacana 40
Joan Baron 16
Stewart Cassidy 38 above and left
Peter Johnson/NHPA 25
Hans Reinhard 30 below
Galen Rowell 44
Leonard Lee Rue III 33 below
Guenter Ziesler 26, 28, 30–31 above, 32–33 above, 34–36, 42, 43, 46–54

The American Lion
Rod Allin/Tom Stack and Associates 62, 64 right
Wolfgang Bayer 70 below
Stephen J. Krasemann/DRK Photo 68
Stephen J. Krasemann/Photo Researchers, Inc. 61, 72
Pat and Tom Leeson/Photo Researchers, Inc. 56
Tom McHugh/Photo Researchers, Inc. 70–71 top two rows
Leonard Lee Rue III 66, 74
Gregory A. Yovan/Tom Stack and Associates 64 above

Prowlers of the North
Rod Allin/Tom Stack and Associates 84, 85
Jack Couffer/Bruce Coleman, Inc. 81
Jean-Paul Ferrero/Jacana 76
Jean-Paul Ferrero and Jean-Michel Labat 92–94
Jean-Paul Ferrero and Jean-Michel Labat/Jacana 90
Warren Garst/Tom Stack and Associates 82
Hans Reinhard 88, 89
Guenter Ziesler 86

Tabby's Relatives
Raimund Cramm/Acaluso International 102 above
Jean-Paul Ferrero 96
Hans Reinhard 101, 102 below, 104, 105
Guenter Ziesler 106

The Leapers
Alain Aigouin/Jacana 120
Erwin and Peggy Bauer/Bruce Coleman, Inc. 117
Jean-Paul Ferrero/Jacana 113
Warren Garst/Tom Stack and Associates 116
Tom McHugh/Photo Researchers, Inc. 114

Index

Numbers in italics indicate pictures